All-Time Favorite Hand-Hooked Rugs:

CELEBRATION'S READERS' CHOICE AWARDS

R·U·G
HOOKING

About the Publisher

Rug Hooking magazine welcomes you to the rug hooking community. Since 1989 *Rug Hooking* has served thousands of rug hookers around the world with its instructional, illustrated articles on dyeing, designing, color planning, hooking techniques, and more. Each issue of the magazine contains color photographs of beautiful rugs old and new, profiles of teachers, designers, and fellow rug hookers, and announcements of workshops, exhibits, and gatherings.

Rug Hooking has responded to its readers' demands for more inspiration and information by establishing an inviting, informative website at *www.rughookingmagazine.com* and by publishing a number of books on this fiber art. Along with how-to pattern books, *Rug Hooking* has produced the competition-based book series *Celebration of Hand-Hooked Rugs*, now in its 20th year, highlighting the incredible art that is being produced today by women and men of all ages.

For more information on rug hooking and *Rug Hooking* magazine, call or write to us at the address below.

Front Cover: *Courting,* designed and hooked by Susan Quicksall. See page 64.

Published by
STACKPOLE BOOKS
5067 Ritter Road
Mechanicsburg, PA 17055
www.stackpolebooks.com

Printed in the United States

10 9 8 7 6 5 4 3 2 1

First edition

Cover design by Caroline Stover
Photography furnished by the artist unless otherwise credited

Library of Congress Cataloging-in-Publication Data

All-time favorite hand-hooked rugs : Celebration's Readers' choice winners / Rug Hooking Magazine.
     p. cm.

ISBN 978-1-881982-70-8
1. Rugs, Hooked. 2. Rugs—History—20th century. 3. Rugs—History—21st century. I. Rug hooking.
NK2807.A45 2010
746.7'4—dc22
2009051066
Canadian GST #R137954772

Contents

Looking Back on Eighteen Years of Readers' Choice

The Gleaners, *page 124.*

*R*ug Hooking magazine has been presenting an annual juried selection of the best hooked rugs created by its readers for two decades. Winners are selected by a jury whose members are usually known for their work as teachers, leaders, or authors within the rug hooking community. The winning rugs are showcased in the elegant publication, *A Celebration of Hand-Hooked Rugs*.

Each year, rug hookers from around the world (generally the United States, Canada, the United Kingdom, and Japan) strive to perfect their skills in the hope of having their work accepted in *Celebration*. Thoughtful effort and hard work goes into the decision to submit a rug for scrutiny by the jury. It takes courage to know you are competing with incredibly talented people from around the world. It takes courage to be able to face the fact your work may not get in. (I am a veteran at receiving *Celebra-*

tion rejections. I am very familiar with the process of waiting for the envelope you hope will be "fat" with the paperwork that accompanies a winning announcement.) Yet, in the face of all these challenges, I think *Celebration* plays an exceedingly important role in the rug hooking world. It allows us to honor and learn from those who have achieved something extraordinary. In addition, it motivates us to master traditional skills, explore new techniques, and fearlessly pursue our own visions of perfection. Significantly, *Celebration* introduces and showcases hooked rug artistry to the rest of the world.

The *Celebration* judging involves two experienced, sophisticated panels of juries. The first is a handful of judges recruited for the task by *Rug Hooking* magazine. The second jury is comprised entirely of *Celebration* readers who are invited to weigh in and select "Readers' Choice" winners. These winners are

J is for Joseph, *page 36.*

featured in a follow-up issue of *Rug Hooking* magazine. Thus, the "Readers' Choice" winners are truly the jewel in the crown since they represent the collective opinions of everyone. And for these winners, being honored and showcased in both *Celebration* and *Rug Hooking* magazine puts their work in a double spotlight that shows the world the loving fruits of their hard labor.

Celebration Through the Years

How has *Celebration* evolved during the course of a generation? What changes have occurred in our use of materials, design preferences, and mastery of color? What are we hooking now, and what were we hooking twenty years ago? How do "Readers' Choice" selections compare with those of the initial jury? These are the questions I asked myself as I poured over a delicious stack of past editions of *Celebration*.

Reviewing eighteen years of past *Celebration* confirmed for me that this annual publication plays a critical role in helping us set increasingly higher goals for our own rug hooking. The rugs just get better and better every year. Designs are more original and complex, and the use of color, more sophisticated.

The most significant changes are in the style, color, and material choices. Burlap, once widely popular, now is used infrequently. We are more adventurous in our use of rich, saturated color. Our color palette is brighter. Pictorial rugs (depicting landscapes, architecture, family gatherings, and seascapes,) are the most popular styles, and are most commonly represented in the category of "original" designs. Richly shaded, classically designed florals and orientals are consistently popular, and are more frequently commercial patterns.

Over the years, we have hooked fewer rugs that are abstract, geometric, or primitive designs although there has been modest growth in primitives and geometrics in recent years. Interestingly, although abstracts are the least represented as *Celebration* winners, renditions of Pearl McGown's "Whirlpool" were chosen three times over the years. But the popularity of abstracts among the judges faded in subsequent years. Designs where the primary emphasis is on living figures (people and animals) have been significantly growing over time, and these designs are most frequently originals.

The format of *Celebration* has changed. *Celebration I* had little discussion about the technical aspects of each rug hooker's piece. Dimension, cut, backing, and material choice, routine information we now see in all photo captions in all *Rug Hooking* magazine publications, were only reported if individual rug hookers included it in their own personal write-ups about their work. Out of 24 featured rugs, only six (25%) were commercial patterns. And there were no separate sections for designs designated as original, commercial, or adaptations. Honorable mention designations were listed, but the rugs not shown. Notably four of the 24 selections were created using materials other than cut wool strips.

By *Celebration III*, construction details (cut, backing, etc.) were more clearly defined and out of 25 rugs, about half were hooked on burlap, but commercial patterns still only comprised 25% of the selections. "Meet the Judges" first appeared in *Celebration IV*, and the number of "winners" was increased to 30. Finally, cut size, backing, and materials were consistently listed for each piece. Commercial patterns and original designs were represented equally. The choice of burlap as a backing, however, predominated only in commercial designs. By *Celebration V*, the editors of *Rug Hooking* magazine made the editorial decision to ensure commercial and original designs were equally represented. Separate headings for "Commercial Designs/Adaptations" and "Original Designs" appeared for the first time and the number of winning selections was equally distributed.

Burlap as the primary backing started to fade from original designs, playing a more significant role only in commercial patterns for a few years. By *Celebration XIII*, burlap was the least popular choice in all selections. Also, by this edition, "Honorable Mention" was given prominent attention with its own gorgeously photographed section. *Celebration* expanded to include 30 "winners" (evenly representing commercial and original patterns) and 20 "honorable mention" selections.

Celebration XV was a watershed. Originals were finally given the most prominent place in the publication. In addition, a features section was added. This features section, over time, has focused on techniques for finishing and photographing rugs, and also showcased "how to" use hooked rugs in home decor.

Readers' Choice

Whether chosen by the initial jury, or through the "Readers' Choice" vote, all of the rugs are uniquely stunning. Every jury has a subjective element to it; we, as judges, are human, and thus our own personal preferences will always play a role in our selections. But what makes a rug stand out to any individual—juror or general reader? What is striking about the "Readers' Choice" selections?

The style of rugs chosen through "Readers' Choice" has been most frequently pictorials, followed by animals, and then florals and orientals. Abstracts have not appeared at all as far as I can tell, and geometrics and primitives played only a modest role. Most significantly, "Readers' Choice" selections are mostly original designs (including designs adapted from family photographs). I reviewed over 120 "Readers' Choice" selections: 41 of them were commercial patterns. Floral and orientals were usually (but not always) commercial patterns. Pictorials and animal designs were usually (but not always) original.

I was fascinated to realize that occasionally "Readers' Choice"

Bamboo, *page 12.*

Waiting for the War Canoes, *page 17.*

selections were "honorable mentions" rather than "winners" picked by the initial jury; three times in *Celebration XIII*, and five times each in *Celebration XIV* and *XV*.

As I reviewed the *Celebration* and the "Readers' Choice" selections, I thought about the role this publication has played in my own thinking about hooked rugs. *Celebration* helped familiarize me with great rugs and their creators at a time when I was first learning about hooked rugs. I was living in St. Louis, Missouri, teaching myself the technical aspects of hooked rug construction, and trying to develop my own creative style. I ran across *Celebrations III*. I loved it so much that I subsequently sought out back copies of numbers I and II. One rug was particularly awe-inspiring, opening new doors to my thinking about what could be created through the medium of rug hooking: Fumiyo Hachisuka's "Bamboo" (*Celebration III*). It remains one of the most strikingly gorgeous hooked rugs I have ever seen. Simple bamboo stalks belie the incredible artistry that went into the rug's design and execution. The fine shading Fumiyo employed was brilliant. Her use of her grandmother's old kimonos for hooking the design added a poignant note. I was not surprised to learn it was also one

of the "Readers' Choice" favorites.

I learned about rug hookers from around the country by pouring over editions of *Celebration*. Certain images made a profound impression. Two rugs that particularly "wowed" me with their design perfection were "J is for Joseph," (designed and hooked by Patty Yoder and featured in *Celebration VI*) and "Rape of Europa" (designed and hooked by Jule Marie Smith, featured in *Celebration VIII*). I admired these masterpieces from my arm chair. I loved learning how Patty developed the color wheel used in "Joseph," through her personal study with Maryanne Lincoln. I loved how Jule chose to depict a Greek myth; I have fond memories of countless hours reading "Bullfinch's Mythology" as a child. It was the personal element of these rug hookers' designs, the part that was based on their own memory of an event (Patty learning to dye wool), or one that evoked my own memories (of loving Greek Mythology) that drew me to their work. And one of the things that made me love Fumiyo's "Bamboo" so much is the fact that she wove her own personal memory into the design by using her grandmother's old kimonos.

I see two themes in "Readers' Choice" selections. The first is process, the focus of most write-ups describing orientals and florals (which tend to be commercial patterns). Carol Ann Scherer, in *Celebration VI*, wrote about her technique in hooking scrolls, and the challenge of dyeing the right shade of Victorian Rose (from a Maryanne Lincoln formula). Carol's winning piece was "Savonnerie," designed by Jane McGown Flynn. Peruse the personal write-ups of all the complex floral and oriental designs and you will see the rug hooker's write up always focuses on describing the process.

The second theme is memory, and a sense of time, place, and personal history. It is associated most frequently with original designs. These "Readers' Choice" original designs are predominantly pictorial or related to pets. As rug hookers and armchair judges, we are drawn to rugs not only because of the brilliance of their execution, but also because of the stories their creators tell us. The design tells a story that we, the viewer, uniquely interpret. But the creator also tells a story with their accompanying personal write-up published in *Celebration*. Do we choose "Readers' Choice" winners solely on visual impact of the design, or are we also influenced by the accompany text telling the back story of each piece? Remember, when the initial jury judges *Celebration* they do not know the stories behind the creation of each piece.

Linda Petech wrote about "Cowscape," in *Celebration I*, describing her memory of pulling off the road and watching three cows in a meadow, and the endearing importance of cows to her beloved Wisconsin landscape. Cathy Henning paid tribute to her mother's family memories with "Tales My Mother Told Me" in *Celebration V*. Bernice Howell's "Best Friends" in XIII is adapted from a 1929 family photograph of her brother and the family dog, on the back step of their Minnesota farm house.

Betty Bouchard's "Waiting for the War Canoes" in *Celebration III* evoked a fond personal memory for me. Betty's write-up spoke about her process of obtaining copyright permission to adapt a painting. But thinking about Betty's process and seeing the picture of her completed piece reminded me of a gorgeous winter day a few years ago. I visited Betty in her cabin home in the woods of northern Vermont. We spent hours talking about her rug hooking, and I got to see most of the body of her work, and learned about her preference for recycled wool. The wood stove was lit, warming her lovely, cozy home. Outside, snow covered the ground and Mr. Bouchard talked about how he tries to ski every day he can. Betty fed us with delicious soup. I went home nourished by good food, great companionship, and spectacular hooked rug art. It was a joy to be reminded of this lovely day as I thought about eighteen years of great hooked rugs.

Take joy in looking at this gorgeous collection of hooked rugs, covering the history of "Readers' Choice" selections from *Celebration*. And let's look forward to many more years of glorious hooked rug art!—*Anne-Marie Littenberg*

Blythe Shoals, *page 112.*

Celebration I—1991

Cowscape, *29¹/₂″ x 38″, wool on monk's cloth. Designed and hooked by Linda Petech, 1991.*

Cowscape
First Place Readers' Choice
Linda Petech

While driving home one day, Linda Petech pulled off the road to watch three cows standing close to a nearby fence. Linda and the cows spent a few minutes looking at each other until one cow, the one on the right, had enough and turned and walked away.

Linda didn't have a camera with her at the time, but the image remained with her and she returned a few days later to draw the scene. She sketched the landscape, but because the cows kept their distance, Linda was forced to rely on imagination, memory, and photographs to design her *Cowscape*.

"To me, these cows are special," Linda says. "In Wisconsin, as with the rest of the country, our small farms are disappearing and quickly being replaced by developments. These Holsteins will live with me for a long time to come." They are a reminder of the bucolic America of our past.

Winter Patterns
Second Place Readers' Choice
Jeanne Fallier

Looking out the window one winter day, Jeanne Fallier eye was drawn to the black-and-white patterns on the tree trunks and branches, in the stream, and in the animal tracks on the snow. The snow-covered bushes brought to mind bowing ballerinas in white tutus as a cardinal pair flew by like a flash of fire. Jeanne put the scene into poetry then transformed the poem into *Winter Patterns*.

Jeanne began by hooking the big tree trunks and the cardinals. Then she climbed the pines to reach their branches, set the branches against the sky and the distant woods, and climbed back down through the hooking until she confronted the squirrel tracks. The shadows on the snow were the hardest, but most important part, to hook.

Jeanne finished this rug over the summer, framed it, and exhibited it at the Chelmsford Art Society, the Massachusetts Council for the Arts, and the Eastern States Exhibition.

Winter Patterns, *22" x 34", wool. Designed and hooked by Jeanne Fallier.*

Into Dreams, *20¹/₂″ in diameter, wool on monk's cloth. Designed and hooked by Jenie Stewart.* CARL LEONARD STEWART

Into Dreams
Third Place Readers' Choice
Jenie Stewart

Carousels are important in Jenie Stewart's life. As a child, her Grandmother Gregson took her to the park in Long Beach, California, to ride the merry-go-round. Years later, on her first date with her later-to-be husband, she returned to that same merry-go-round.

Into Dreams, which took Jenie three months to complete, began as many of her designs do—at the drafting table in her basement workshop. First drawn on artist's tissue, she transferred the pattern to monk's cloth. She tried to see how small the piece could be and still be hooked successfully. The girl's face is only 1¹/₂″ x 1¹/₄″, and the saddle and trappings on the pony are very small and detailed.

Jenie selected the colors and dyed the fabric, which she enjoyed almost as much as the hooking. She used Dorr's white and natural wool, and hand dyed the fabric with formulas from *Anyone Can Dye for Making Rugs* by Clarisse Cox and *Shading Swatches* by Clarisse McLain. She also referred to Joan Moshimer's *Jacobean Formulas* and *Imari Formulas*.

The hardest part to hook was the feather in the child's right hand. Jenie wanted it to look light and fluffy, and she struggled to get it just right. She re-hooked it so many times that she thought the monk's cloth would fall apart before she finally succeeded.

Into Dreams is the first in a series of three original designs that Jenie had planned for *The Dream Series*. Together they portray the happiness of a child in the night. In 1990, *Into Dreams* won a first place blue ribbon in the wall hangings category at the Kansas State Fair.

Butch, *34" x 45", wool. Designed and hooked by Betty Jean Vogan, 1990. © California Dreamers and Recycled Paper Products, Inc. All rights reserved. Reprinted by permission.*

Butch

Betty Jean Vogan

When Betty Jean Vogan sees an interesting picture or idea, her first thought is that she wants to hook it. It was just that way with *Butch*. Betty Jean saw the poster of an adorable little boy with his bag packed, ready to head out into the world by himself, and she knew it would make a wonderful rug. The teddy bear, the holes in the knees of his pants, and the look in his eyes give this portrait character.

Betty Jean enjoyed hooking the tennis shoes the most. She was very careful to make sure that the laces were a little dirty in some spots. The jacket was a pleasure to hook: she used three different plaid wools. She used both spot dyeing and swatches for the rest of the hooking. Betty Jean found that using whatever materials she had available often worked the best.

Celebration II—1992

Four Seasons, *20" x 67" (each panel), wool. Designed and hooked by Thelma Kubiak, Wintzville, Missouri, 1986.*

Four Seasons
First Place Readers' Choice
Thelma Kubiak

The inspiration for Thelma Kubiak's piece was the St. Louis phone book. The springtime panel in Thelma's rug hooking is an adaptation of artist Gary Lucy's cover. The other three panels illustrate the other seasons. The center field is wheat: green in spring, then golden. On the bottom, she added blackberries that she and her friends picked as children. The birds and some leaves were hooked from swatches. Rows of cedar were

hooked with three or four plaids to make different shades, and the fields and the lake were several shades of spot dye. Lots of materials came straight from the ragbag. This was Thelma's first experience hooking with plaids and spot dye.

While hooking *The Four Seasons,* Thelma would often drive to St. Louis, a three-and-a half-hour trip, to hook with Mary Melvin.

Michelle, *3' x 5', wool on monk's cloth. Designed and hooked by Sibyl Osicka, Parma, Ohio, 1990.*

Michelle
Second Place Readers' Choice
Sibyl Osicka

As the years go by, members of Sibyl Osicka's family ask, "When are you going to hook something for me?" If they keep after her long enough, and she has enough time, she admits that something will usually get done. That's exactly how her daughter Michelle ended up with this rug, named for her. The drawing is original, as are all the dye formulas.

The large rose in the center of the medallion is the focal point of the rug. Roses mean love, and she thought there was no better way to let her daughter know how she felt. She placed calla lilies in the arrangements, and added scrolls in all four corners. After teaching and liking the cross-hatching at a McGown Southern Workshop, Sibyl incorporated some cross-hatching on all four sides of the rug.

Bamboo, *4½' x 6½', wool and silk. Designed and hooked by Fumiyo Hachisuka, Suginami-ku, Tokyo, Japan, 1991.*

Bamboo
Third Place Readers' Choice
Fumiyo Hachisuka

Fumiyo Hachisuka was introduced to rug hooking while she was living in Toronto in the late 1970s. She visited a rug hooking display in a library and was drawn to this unfamiliar art form. She sought out someone to teach her, and learned the techniques and fine points of hooking with other Japanese fiber artists who lived in the area. She studied with Fannie Sinclair while her daughters were in school.

She returned to Japan in 1983. With no rug hooking community in Japan to support her in Tokyo, she relied on books to guide her, and eventually finished her first original piece in 1985. She began to teach, and now conducts regular classes and holds an annual exhibition of students' work in downtown Tokyo. Her twentieth show was held in the fall of 2009.

Fumiyo considers rug hooking's connection to recycling to be one of its attractions. She used that aspect to introduce the craft to others who are concerned about waste in the environment. Hooking rugs in one of many ways to reduce fabric trash.

Her statement about *Bamboo* explains her stand. "It is wonderful to make a fine work with new, dyed wool cloths, and on the other hand, it is a miracle to change the old used clothes which are destined to be thrown away into beautiful works, treasuring our limited precious natural resources of the earth. That is why I used my grandmother's old kimonos to make the original design I displayed there, *Bamboo*."

Sun Dance, *54" x 54", wool. Designed and hooked by Pamela J. Smith, Miami, Florida, 1991.*

Sun Dance
Best of Show Readers' Choice
Pamela J. Smith

Pamela J. Smith designed this piece for the Sun Dance Institute in Utah. The Sun Dance was the one time each year when all the Native American tribes got together to settle differences, celebrate rites of manhood, and look to the future.

Pamela comes from the Oklahoma territory and her piece represents her heritage. Rug hooking for Pamela is not a craft but a way of life, an expression of what lives inside her. When words fail and life—or her checking account—doesn't make sense any more, she can sit down at her frame and make something from nothing, and at that moment there is a wonderful feeling of accomplishment.

Most Indian tribes had a tradition of the "give away," when a person took a most prized possession and gave it away. When that happened, one's past life was gone and life began anew. "Each of us holds something precious that relates to the piece of ground we come from. I want to pass that on to my children. In every loop of the *Sun Dance* I put a thought, some memory about my family's joys and sorrows. And when the *Sun Dance* goes to hang in the Sun Dance Institute in Utah, a piece of my past will live forever."

Celebration III—1993

Spanky's Fish Ride, *47" x 32", #6-cut wool on linen. Designed and hooked by Florence Petruchik, Windham Center, Connecticut, 1991.* WILLIAM M. BISHOP

Spanky's Fish Ride
First Place Readers' Choice

Florence Petruchik

Florence Petruchik's goal is to hook rugs for all of her grandchildren. With *Spanky's Fish Ride*, she is six rugs into that goal. This original design was created for her grandson, Pete. The idea for *Spanky's Fish Ride* came from an old colonial weather vane that featured a fish with a flag coming out of the top. She decided to have her grandson Pete riding the fish and holding the flag. Armed with that fun concept, the rest of the rug developed around her center theme, and *Spanky's Fish Ride* was launched. "It's a rug I hope gives Pete as much pleasure when he's telling his grandchildren about it as it's given me making it for him," says Florence.

Soul Melody, *36" x 24" #4- and 5-cut wool on linen. Designed and hooked by Kathleen L. Russell, Carlisle, Pennsylvania, 1992.* WILLIAM M. BISHOP

Soul Melody
Second Place Readers' Choice
Kathleen L. Russell

Nothing has ever given Kathleen Russell the feeling of calm and connectedness that she had while riding through the Pennsylvania countryside when she was a child. In *Soul Melody*, she wanted to recreate that special feeling. Technically, her goal was to experiment with her speed-tufting tool and to make color sing by mixing like values of different colors, thus using color in a more painterly manner.

"The patterned succession of the checks and of the trees in *Soul Melody* represents the music in me, passed on to me from my mother," Kathleen says. "The rug also symbolizes the artistic soul connection between my father and me." Kathleen's father was a retired architect and artist who underwent brain surgery the year preceding his death. For eight months, while her hooked piece was coming to life, Kathleen and her father were able to meet regularly to share a spiritual renewal from the country landscape.

The color in Kathleen's work is the result of years of exposure to the creativity of both parents and their passionate love of art. And while she admits it might sound sentimental, she tells viewers of the finished rug to "behold the melody of my soul."

Kathleen dedicated *Soul Melody* to her parents.

Waiting for the War Canoes, *23" x 30" plus fringe, #3- and 4-cut wool on monk's cloth. Adapted from an oil painting by William Robinson Leigh. Designed and hooked by Betty Bouchard, Richmond, Vermont, 1992.*
WILLIAM M. BISHOP

Waiting for the War Canoes
Third Place Readers' Choice
Betty Bouchard

Betty Bouchard prefers to work with whatever materials she has on hand from 14 years of collecting skirts and slacks, occasionally adding a few yards of purchased, off-white wool. For *Waiting for the War Canoes*, she spot dyed the wool for the cradleboard and the light parts of the sky. Other wool pieces were simmered together in a light wash to marry the colors, and many were used as-is. She then hooked the rug in her usual trial-and-error method.

While Betty understands that some rug hookers believe that rugs should only be hooked for the floor—practical, but pretty, as perhaps the first rug makers intended—she doesn't always agree. "Little could those pioneers of the craft have dreamed how their attempt to put some comfort and color into their lives would grow into what I believe has become an art form today—one that's perfectly appropriate hung on the wall," she says.

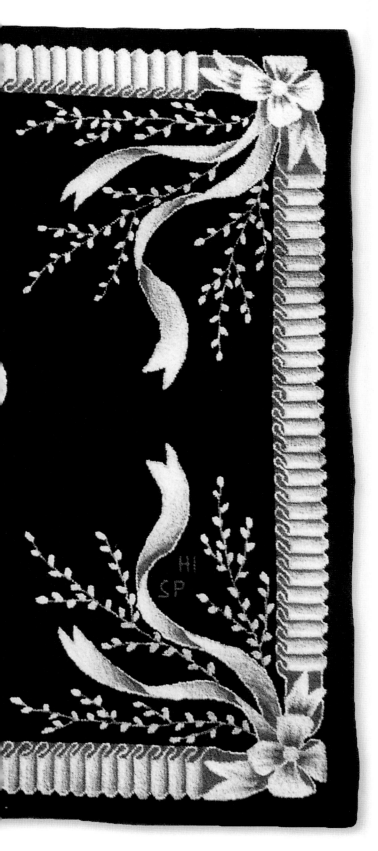

Victorian Flowers
Best of Show Readers' Choice
Ingrid Hieronimus

Ingrid Hieronimus designed *Victorian Flowers* for a rug hooking teacher's workshop. Rug hookers past and present have always loved to hook flowers, and Ingrid is no exception.

In the Victorian era, flowers were everywhere—in wreaths, bouquets, and garlands—and were used in decoration on everything: bell pulls, carpets, curtain ties, cushions, chair seats, wallpaper, ornate furniture, and knick-knacks. This overabundance of flowers could make a room quite overwhelming and busy. Ribbons were very popular and they went well with the floral décor. Baby's breath was a favorite, giving a wispy effect.

The ribbon Ingrid used as the frame, or border, flows around the flowers, adding weight to the edge of the rug. The border was adapted from a needlepoint pattern. Ingrid substituted pussy willow for the baby's breath. The pussy willows and ribbons flow out of the corners to direct the viewer's eye to the center flowers. Still wispy, the pussy willows fill in the otherwise blank, potentially uninteresting corners.

The background is textured black wool overdyed with dark green, following the tradition of dark backgrounds found in the Victorian era. Ingrid used swatches for the flowers, leaves, and ribbons, and she spot dyed wool for the veins and the outline of the ribbon.

Victorian Flowers, *55" x 42", #3- and 4-cut wool on monk's cloth. Designed and hooked by Ingrid Hieronimus, Petersburg, Ontario, Canada, 1992.* WILLIAM M. BISHOP

Celebration IV—1994

L is for Lydia, *33" x 45", #6-cut wool on burlap. Designed and hooked by Patty Yoder, Tinmouth, Vermont, 1993.* WILLIAM M. BISHOP

L is for Lydia
First Place Readers' Choice
Patty Yoder

Patty Yoder loves to hook sheep, and she decided to hook "Lydia" (named after a great aunt with similar features) after receiving permission from the sheep's owner to capture her on film. *L is for Lydia* is just one of a series of sheep rugs Patty has planned.

Patty started this wall hanging in 1993 at Green Mountain Rug School in Elizabeth Black's animal course. Elizabeth taught Patty to look at the light and shadow and to study her photograph to determine which highlights and shadows were important. Patty is especially proud of the deep shadow underneath Lydia that she hooked with an over-dyed tweed.

Patty enlisted the help of colorist Maryanne Lincoln to dye Lydia's wool. They used the stove-top method and took a casual approach, dyeing by eye. Patty used new, white wool for most of the rug, but she did hook one tweed into the border and over dye another with black and green for the background.

Patty loves Lydia's face, especially the eyes because "you *have* to think about what *she's* thinking." Patty faced several challenges: The legs and hooves were hard to hook realistically, but after several attempts she succeeded. The trees in the background were difficult: Patty hooked strips in the trees in different directions for a bushy effect. In fact, she didn't hook a single portion of the rug in straight rows—even the straw underneath Lydia's face, the grass, and the lines of the fence are not straight.

Sanctuary
Second Place Readers' Choice
Betty Young

When Betty Young couldn't find a special piece of artwork to hang over the fireplace in her new cottage on Lake Chautauqua in New York, she decided to hook a wall hanging for herself. Given the setting of the cottage, Betty thought *Sanctuary* was an appropriate design, and because she had never hooked a pictorial, she thought it would be a good learning experience.

With the help of her teacher from the Chautauqua Rug School, Helen Connelly, Betty devised a color plan. Helen provided formulas for dyeing new swatches and over dyeing spots, plaids, and checks, and she taught Betty how to combine the colored wool as she hooked feathers, trees, and water.

At Helen's suggestion, Betty painted the sky by brushing dye solutions onto white wool with a paintbrush. After brushing the wool, she sprinkled salt on it, rolled it in tin foil, and simmered it to set the dye. Then she hooked the sky horizontally as it came off her cutter. Betty said, "I really felt like an artist as I 'painted' from my palette of colored wools."

Betty particularly likes the three-dimensional mallards and the subdued sky. She found it difficult to hook realistic heads, so she used photographs as visual aids. And she studied trees during leisurely drives through Chautauqua to make sure her trees looked as real as possible.

Betty learned several new techniques while hooking *Sanctuary*. She learned how to hook realistic trees, realistic water, and realistic reflections. Dyeing wool with a paintbrush was a new technique for her as well. Apparently, the technique was successful; visitors to Betty's home often look at *Sanctuary* and think that it is a painting.

Sanctuary, *30" x 24", #3-cut wool on burlap. Designed by Jane McGown Flynn; hooked by Betty Young, Akron, Ohio, 1993.* WILLIAM M. BISHOP

William Morris
Third Place Readers' Choice
Kay Forbush

William Morris is named for an English designer of the Victorian era. Morris worked at the dawn of industrialization when mass-production was coming into vogue, and he was well known for his unique wallpaper patterns, textiles, silverware, and pottery. This rug is adapted from Morris' last wallpaper design, *Compton*. Morris detested machine-made products, so Kay Forbush thinks he would enjoy the adaptation of his design into a handcrafted medium.

Kay hooked *William Morris* because she considers this design one of the loveliest patterns available today. She admires the way it "interweaves and overlaps, forming three distinct pattern layers" that create a three-dimensional effect.

Kay devised her own color plan for the rug. For the background, she over dyed light blue wool with a blue-gray dye, intentionally keeping it uneven to make the background interesting. The large main flowers were hooked with dip-dyed wool; each petal changing from light gold to golden brown on the outside and from light peach to a brownish mahogany on the inside. The white secondary flowers and the leaves are shaded with swatches that give the flowers an open, lacy feel. Kay tucked short bits of the main flower colors into the stylized leaves in the border.

The placement of highlight and shadow is the most important component of a shaded design. She checked portions of the rug in different lights and times of day as she proceeded to make sure that she achieved the affect she was after.

Kay finished *William Morris* in nine months, and it was exhibited at Kay's local guild show in the spring of 1993. *William Morris* lies in Kay's living room underneath a glass coffee table.

William Morris, *31" x 44", #3-cut wool on burlap. Designed by Jane McGown Flynn; hooked by Kay Forbush, Middleburg Heights, Ohio, 1993.* WILLIAM M. BISHOP

Game Preserve, *10'6" x 7', #3- and 4-cut wool on cotton rug warp. Adapted from Edith Dana's design and hooked by Cheryl G. W. Orcutt, Peterborough, New Hampshire, 1994.* WILLIAM M. BISHOP

Game Preserve
Best of Show Readers' Choice
Cheryl G. W. Orcutt

Cheryl G. W. Orcutt likens *Game Preserve* to a Puccini opera. Act I—the center—is light and melodious. In Act II, the complexities of the plot unfold. The border is Act III—heavy with karma and the final resolution. In the end, she says, the rug is the sum of its parts that must work together to achieve that enigmatic and elusive magic.

Cheryl wasn't even thinking about her next project when teacher Hallie Hall presented her with an old pattern on which *Game Preserve* is based, but she immediately fell in love with the piece. Together they transferred the design onto a new backing and adapted it to suit Cheryl's taste. The original design was inspired by Audubon drawings, so the addition of wildflowers and leaves suited the rug perfectly.

Cheryl and Hallie worked on the color plan together. Cheryl spent many hours studying the design, and the color plan evolved slowly as Cheryl worked on different elements in the rug.

Cheryl did all the dyeing herself, using extra-heavy wool to ensure a long life for the rug. She used almost every dyeing technique known, and the result is a symphony of colors. The background alone is a "harmony of turquoise, lavender, magenta, blue-green, green-blue, sea-green, here a loop of yellow, there a loop of purple." She even invented a modified jar-dyeing technique to create spotty gradation swatches for several parts of the rug.

The female pheasant was hooked last, and it's Cheryl's favorite part of the rug. It was also her biggest challenge because she didn't want it to look like a "brown blob." Cheryl used a variety of subtle colors including blue and rose to bring the pheasant to life.

Cheryl hooked *Game Preserve* in about 18 months. To help it wear better, she added a buttonhole knot to each whipping stitch on the edge; the knot takes the pressure off the rug, protecting the fragile edge. During the early stages of the rug, a friend saw it and bought it for his country house. The birds now inhabit his library.

Celebration V—1995

Tales My Mother Told Me, *56" x 51", #3- and 6-cut wool on burlap. Designed and hooked by Catherine Henning, Burlington, Ontario, 1994.*

Tales My Mother Told Me
First Place Readers' Choice—Original Design
Catherine Henning

This rug pays tribute to family memories from the family homestead in Ontario. The rug depicts 10 separate stories. The lawn shows Uncle Charlie as a ghost scaring his sisters, a water fight between him and Catherine's mother, and the tent where her Aunt Mary died of tuberculosis. In the barnyard, a gander chases her mother while Gramma beheads a chicken. Grampa hurries to help Uncle Charlie as he is gored by a bull. The girls' bareback ride ends when the horse decides to take a drink at the river. Aunt Sue, sitting too far forward, takes an

unexpected spill into the water. Mother is busy in the fields, tending the sheep and moving the hay.

The rug's border contains the family names. The thistle flag of Scotland, the crown, and the maple leaf, recall Catherine's Scottish ancestors. The gems and the band in the crown are color coded to the children's names and figures in the rug. Catherine dyed and over dyed some of the wool, incorporating some special recycled wool. The maple leaves are hooked with MacLean tartan.

Ellendale, 33" x 22", #3-cut wool on linen. Designed and hooked by Betty A. Jacobs, Silver Spring, Maryland, 1994.

Ellendale
Second Place Readers' Choice—Original Design
Betty A. Jacobs

Betty Jacobs always hooks original designs, sometimes from photographs, sometimes straight from her imagination—and often a little of both. Her inspiration for *Ellendale* was a photograph she took in Ellendale, Delaware. When the film was developed, she knew she had to hook a rug based on the photo.

She enlarged the photo on a copy machine, drew the design on paper, traced the design to pattern stock, then to linen. Betty followed the colors in the photo to color plan her rug. She used a variety of wool—old, new, as is, and dyed. She dyed some of her own and used other dyed pieces from Marie Azzaro, including a piece of tan wool with a green streak that was just made for the boards on the porch. Her scrunch-dyed wool gives the irregular colors that make the wall hanging realistic and vibrant. Betty enjoyed hooking the roof and the chrysanthemums, which she said "almost hooked themselves." She hooked with a #3 cut, which let her concentrate on elaborate and realistic detail.

Boldt's Yacht-House, *66" x 46", #4- and 6-cut wool on rug warp. Designed and hooked by Prudence Matthews, Binghamton, New York, 1994.*

Boldt's Yacht-House
Third Place Readers' Choice—Original Design
Prudence Matthews

Prudence Matthews started hooking George Boldt's yacht-house in November 1993. Boldt was a German immigrant who made his fortune working at the Waldorf Astoria. He built a castle on an island for his wife, who died before the work was completed. The yacht-house was part of his estate and is one of the few of its type still standing in the United States—architectural students often come to study the building's design.

Prudence had spent much of the previous summer taking photos of the island in order to, as she explains it, be fairly accurate but impressionistic at the same time. Roslyn Logdon's lessons on shading, light, and dimension helped Prudence achieve her goals.

Prudence found the trees to be difficult. She wanted to show how the wind blows across the river and catches the tree branches, but she says, "the little girl in me just wanted to create Christmas trees." She ripped the trees out over and over until she succeeded.

The rocks were her greatest challenge. Prudence took a mini-geology course to learn about the varying colors, shapes, and tex-

tures of rocks. As with the trees, Prudence ripped out her rocks' loops many times and started again. She used undyed tweeds and herringbones to create texture.

Claire DeRoos helped Prudence dye wool for the water and sky, but much of the rug is undyed, textured wool. "Hooking is like a miracle," says Prudence. She loves using a variety of textured and dyed wools, not knowing what the effect will be until she is done.

The boats—a staple in all of Prudence's rugs featuring the Thousand Islands—are her favorite design element, mainly because she grew up on the water. Her grandfather built a summer home there in 1907, and she has always loved the natural beauty and historic sites of the area. In her rugs, Prudence captures the Islands' scenic beauty and Victorian charm.

Prudence worked on *Boldt's Yacht-House* for a year. Her rugs cover the floors and walls of her summer home.

Harmony, *35" x 70", #3-cut wool on monk's cloth. Designed by Jane McGown Flynn; hooked by Suzanne Petty, Kingwood, Texas, 1994.*

Harmony
First Place Readers' Choice—Commercial Design
Suzanne Petty

*H*armony was chosen by Suzanne's youngest daughter, Andrea, the only child in the family who did not receive a hooked rug from Suzanne's mother before her death. Andrea loved leaf scrolls and flowers, and because music is important in her life, she was especially excited by the name of this rug. Suzanne agreed to hook the rug, only to discover that it would be the largest project she had ever attempted.

"Brimming with confidence," Suzanne took the project to the Texas Rug Camp. Due to a bout with polio after she was married in 1952, Suzanne does not have enough strength in her arms to dye wool, so teacher Lois Dugal helped out. Lois dyed all of the wool for the flowers and the greenery, based on paint swatches from Suzanne.

Suzanne finished the center before the next year's camp. Again, Lois was there to lend a hand. The scroll was the most exciting part of the rug; she worked to keep it in harmony without exactly matching the sides. She repeated colors throughout to make the parts similar but not identical. The scroll was Suzanne's most dramatic learning experience, learning to incorporate different greens into one design element.

Because she used a #3 cut, Suzanne took longer to complete the rug than she expected. She finished it during the summer of 1994 while recuperating from a broken leg. The rug has won a blue ribbon, a best-of-show ribbon, and a special rug award ribbon at the Texas State Fair.

Esther's Oriental, *120" x 144", #5- to 7-cut wool on linen. Adapted from several Persian rugs and hooked by Esther R. Jackson, Warwick, Rhode Island, 1993.*

Esther's Oriental
Second Place Readers' Choice—Commercial Design
Esther R. Jackson

Esther modeled this design after several Persian rugs and oriental borders. She used eight large, felt-tipped pens to put her pattern on linen backing; it took a week of eight-hour days to completely transfer the design. Esther added more than 12 different roses and peonies, her favorite elements in the rug, to the pattern.

With the pattern drawn, Esther started hooking the center with white wool she had been saving in a cedar chest for a special project. After hooking some flowers, she wanted to move on to the background, but she didn't want it to be all white. However, all of her dyes were in Rhode Island; the only thing available to dye with was tea. So Esther boiled tea bags in a Dutch oven, added the

wool, and let the color seep into the fabric. When the color had set, she added vinegar to fix the color and let the wool dry outside in the sun.

Esther had a piece of medium turquoise Dorr wool. She also had 10 pounds of off-white wool, acquired over many years. She decided to use as-is wool for the outside border, with the smaller border hooked in a bright turquoise over dyed with brown.

The roses, peonies, and leaves are dyed with many pastels and white, using formulas form the book *Anyone Can Dye*. Esther used Joan Moshimer's Imar Gold I formula to dye the golds over white, light gold, and beige wool. She also dyed five, 4-ounce skeins of yarn for whipping the edges and for the fringe.

Ancient Wall, *17″ x 25″, #3-cut wool on burlap. Adapted from a photograph in the Minneapolis Tribune and hooked by Bernice Howell, Beltsville, Maryland, 1994.*

Ancient Wall
Third Place Readers' Choice—Commercial Design
Bernice Howell

Arches have always captured Bernice's attention. In her eyes, arches—in cathedrals, in bridges, or anywhere—"fit the poet's expression 'a thing of beauty is a joy forever.'" A picture of an ancient Turkish wall in the travel section of the Sunday paper captured her imagination. Her husband made a slide of that photo so that Bernice could project the image onto the wall and transfer the design onto burlap.

This was Bernice's first hooked piece, worked primarily in shades of beige. She used tweeds, plaids, and heathers to mimic the rough hand-hewn stones. Most of the wool came from her ever-growing collection from thrift shops. She used much of the fabric as is, but she did purchase and spot dye a hound's-tooth check.

The wall on the left was Bernice's greatest challenge. She found herself doing some situational dyeing, using scarlet, cocoa brown, and caramel over beige to darken the wall as she hooked upward. She used a #3 cut because it was easier on her hand and wrist, and she liked the appearance and detail that a fine cut of wool allowed. Hooking the areas that were shaded from the sun was difficult; the colors had to change enough to show the difference, yet not be obvious. She was pleased with the final results.

Celebration VI—1996

Earthly Delights
First Place Readers' Choice— Original Design

Lucy Clark

Sometimes rugs don't turn out as planned. Lucy Clark started with an image of her husband, George, picking tomatoes in his vegetable garden. Her teacher, Mary Sheppard Burton, encouraged Lucy to enlarge the design and include other elements of the Clarks' country home. George is still the focal point of the design, but the scene now includes a shed encircled with flowers, and distant trees and mountains.

Lucy felt overwhelmed by the size of the rug and the design challenges. Mary was a great help, especially with choosing the basic green dyes for the background. "I learned more about green than I imagined possible," Lucy says, "and I still don't know enough." Lucy dye painted the blue wool for the sky. She hooked most of the mountains and tree trunks from recycled wools. A herringbone edge was used to bind the rug, with a heather effect created by using three colors of yarn.

Although Lucy has some near vision impairment, it has not decreased her creativity nor affected her use of color. "I don't know how to describe my work, but I can say that I love color, the adventure of dyeing wool, and the feel of the materials in my hands." She says she still has a lot to learn and appreciates the knowledge that she gains from each new project.

Lucy's favorite part of *Earthly Delights* is George with his garden cart and basket, and the shed surrounded by flowers. She proudly claims the hooked figure really looks like George.

Earthly Delights, *60" x 43", #4- and 5-cut wool on linen. Designed and hooked by Lucy Clark, Fairfax, Virginia, 1995.*

J is for Joseph, *34" x 31", #6-cut wool on burlap. Designed and hooked by Patty Yoder, Tinmouth, Vermont, 1995.*

J is for Joseph
Second Place Readers' Choice—Original Design
Patty Yoder

As Patty Yoder worked on this installment of her sheep rugs, she attended the Texas Rug Hooking Camp where colorist Maryanne Lincoln was teaching one of her many workshops on dyeing. Maryanne advised Patty to work on her own to "create an inner color wheel using formulas that followed along with percentages of the contrasting colors." In other words, Patty would select opposite colors—for example, red and green—and use either $2/3$ red with $1/3$ green for the dye solution, or vice versa.

Patty dyed about 18 colors in 8" x 12" pieces, using Maryanne's formulas. When she saw all of the colors displayed together in a row, she thought, "Gee, that looks like a coat of many colors," referring to the biblical story of Joseph and his colorful coat. Since

Patty had already completed nine sheep named after letters of the alphabet, *J is for Joseph* was the obvious title for this rainbow-colored sheep.

Each color in the rug blends into the one that follows it in the color wheel, with a few variations here and there. Hooking the body of the sheep was the most enjoyable part, and it certainly never became boring with the variety of hues she had to work with.

The border presented a challenge: how could it blend with the design, yet be noticeably different for contrast and visual interest? Patty used a verse around the border: the violet letters lie against a striped background that repeats the rainbow colors of the animal.

Glynis
Third Place Readers' Choice— Original Design
Della Griffiths

Della Griffiths is lucky to have such an accommodating family dog. She persuaded Glynis, a West Highland terrier, to pose for a photograph in a Victorian child's chair usually reserved for dolls. Glynis cooperated like a pro.

Glynis was hooked with as-is, over-dyed, and dip-dyed wool. The wool for the dog was dip dyed beginning with TOD #149 gray solution over Dorr's white wool. As the gray was depleted, Della added Seal Brown by the spoonful. She continued this technique until she had wool that progressed from gray to brown, with all the values in between. She did not use all the values of these colors, but enough of a range to create the shadows in Glynis's pure white coat.

The wool for the ears was dyed pink, then over dyed with some of the same gray. Gray over dyed with green also found its way into the leaves. Fuzzy, as-is wool was used for the thistles. Because the piece was to be used as a wall hanging, the wool for these prickly plants was puffed up to look more authentic. Della achieved the hairy look of the dog's coat by using narrow pieces of wool, some hooked beyond the dog's outline, for a wispy effect.

Della's favorite part of this piece is Glynis herself. The border was difficult. The trick was to make it interesting, but not so interesting that it would draw attention away from Glynis. To unite the border and the center, Della hooked parts of the chair out into the border, which successfully gave the rug more dimension.

Glynis, *23" x 37", #3- and 4-cut wool on linen. Designed and hooked by Della Griffiths, Glenshaw, Pennsylvania.*

Salute to Kennebunkport, *38" x 39", #6-cut wool on monk's cloth. Adapted from a painting and hooked by Emily Robertson, formerly Emily Erickson, Mequon, Wisconsin.*

Salute to Kennebunkport
First Place Readers' Choice—Commercial Design

Emily Robertson

When she first began hooking, Emily Robertson used wide #8-cut wool. As she honed her rug hooking skills, however, she found that a #6 cut better suited her painterly style. Like a painter, she decides on color and composition as a project progresses, making adjustments as she goes.

This rug is from a painting of a scene from Kennebunkport, Maine, that she saw in a magazine. Emily color planned the rug with the help of her teacher, Carol Kassera, who also helped her to dye the wool. About 90% of the piece was hooked with new wool, most of it over dyed. The combined efforts of Carol and Emily resulted in a piece that dances with color.

Emily loved the challenge of continually adjusting the texture and balance of color. The only problem she encountered was hooking the figure of the woman. She had to tear it out and re-hook it several times before she was satisfied. Her finished rug reflects the sparkle of summer in Kennebunkport.

American Express Train, *36" x 22¹/₂", #3-cut wool on burlap. Designed by Heirloom; hooked by Marjorie Clinton, Hopedale, Massachusetts, 1994.*

American Express Train
Second Place Readers' Choice—Commercial Design
Marjorie Clinton

Marjorie Clinton chose this Heirloom pattern to remind her of all the wonderful times she and her late husband spent riding trains together. They rode nearly every train within 300 miles of their home and collected all sorts of train memorabilia. With this pattern, Marjorie says she "just had to ride one more train with my hook."

A Currier & Ives print served as a reference for the train's colors. Much of the wool Marjorie used was left over from other creations. And she had bags of scraps donated to her by older ladies who had retired from hooking rugs. Marjorie and her teacher, Diane Stoffel, enjoyed poking through the bags, searching for just the right colors. The only dyeing Marjorie did was for the sky.

Hooking the engine was the most enjoyable part of the project for Marjorie, but also the most problematic. It was difficult to hook the many small parts of the engine and give form to the round sections. But she persevered and achieved an almost photographic realism. She created the look of metal on the train by using complementary colors next to each other to simulate the metallic shine.

Marjorie confesses that "it really is difficult for me to pick a

favorite part of the rug because I'm so pleased with it all. I do love the way the smoke looks, and the hillside and the tree. But the engine, I suppose, would have to be my favorite."

Savonnerie

Third Place Readers' Choice—
Commercial Design

Carol Anne Scherer

Carol Ann Scherer is especially fond of tapestry hooking because the floral designs go so well with the many pieces of Victorian furniture her family has inherited. The motifs of flowers and scrolls in these designs remind her of the fine shading in crewel embroidery, another fiber art that she enjoys.

Savonnerie, a beautiful, delicate, Jane McGown Flynn design, appealed to Carol so much that she was compelled to take wool in hand and create a rug of her own. The spiral ribbons in the center diamond, the bow and trailing ribbon in the center bouquet, and the feathery scrolls all reminded her of the floral designs in paintings by the Dutch masters.

Ellen Femiano, Carol's instructor, helped with the color planning. Fond of the country look, Carol chose Maryanne Lincoln's Country Colors collection of wool. Victorian Rose was perfect for the roses in the corner sections, and she chose Light Plum for the center roses. Carol dyed the wool for the leaves with one of Maryanne's formulas for green.

Carol particularly enjoyed "hooking the diamond spiral, as it really set off the rug and led to each of the other points of interest." Having disciplined herself to concentrate on either scrolls or flowers in her other pieces, Carol was thrilled to watch each section of this rug develop as she brought together those hard-earned skills. Carol hooked the feathery scrolls with a transition swatch that went from dark beige to pink, giving the scrolls an airy, fluid quality.

Savonnerie, *39" x 63", #3-cut wool on monk's cloth. Designed by Jane McGown Flynn; hooked by Carol Anne Scherer, Dayton, Maryland, 1995.*

M. Monet in His Water Garden
First Place Readers' Choice—Original Design
Dorothy Pope

In preparation for this piece, Dorothy Pope researched Monet's life and studied biographical sketches and photographs of him and his wonderful water garden at Giverny, France. When she began sketching, she started with the willows and the water lilies, using the flowers in her backyard pond as models.

When she finally began to hook, she followed the advice of her resident consultant—her husband—who told her start with Claude. Then she moved on to the bridge, some irises and lilies, and "the rest just followed," Dorothy says. Color planning was minimal because she used colors that would have occurred naturally in the scene. "The color of the Japanese bridge is close to that of his real bridge," Dorothy says, "and he really did have a pink boat, though the shape is not authentic."

Although the colors suggested themselves, selecting the correct values was a continual challenge. Dorothy's creative use of fabrics garnered from many sources helped. "As usual I incorporated a number of plaids and textured pieces, and my collection of greens was severely drained," she says. "A green, black, and gold hound's-tooth check was ugly as a jacket, but positively perfect as foliage. . ." Look at the tree in the upper left corner.

Creating Monet's reflection in the water was difficult. Dorothy wanted it to look natural, but not too prominent. She hooked it, ripped it out, and hooked it again until she was satisfied. The verse is one that Dorothy believes has been attributed to Monet. She finished the edges by whipstitching yarn over cording. Then she handstitched a fabric binding, rather than rug tape, to the edges and the back. The rug is long and narrow, designed to fit in a hallway.

M. Monet in His Water Garden, *30" x 98", #3-, 4-, and 5-cut wool and wool blends on monk's cloth. Designed and hooked by Dorothy Pope, Gladstone, Oregon, 1996.* MICHAEL SLADE

Hibiscus, Hibiscus, *72" x 48", #5-cut wool on monk's cloth. Designed by Richard and Georgianne Bugdal; hooked by Georgianne Bugdal, Miami, Florida, 1996.*

Hibiscus, Hibiscus
Second Place Readers' Choice—Original Design
Georgianne Bugdal

Georgianne Bugdal took the suggestion of her husband, Richard, when she wanted to hook a rug reminiscent of their Miami home. A rug incorporating hibiscus flowers was the obvious choice, since their home is surrounded by many hibiscus varieties. Richard, a graphic designer, suggested they make the flowers large and he drew the outline of six hibiscus blossoms directly on monk's cloth.

Georgianne used all new wool, some of which was dip dyed by Anne Eastwood. She also used swatches from previous projects, and some from wool dyeing experiments that came out mottled. The pink was as-is new wool.

Hooking such large blossoms was a considerable undertaking, and as Georgianne began *Hibiscus, Hibiscus,* she realized quickly that she didn't have enough experience with shading. So she

ripped out what she had done and set the pattern aside. Five years later, after classes in fine shading with Connie Charleson and many weekend classes with B.J. Andreas and Anne Eastwood, she took up the project again.

Although she used a #5 cut, the shading was as complex as with a #3 because of the large size. "Working with 12 or more values of one color in such a large flower helped," she says. Georgianne unashamedly admits that her favorite part of the rug is "the fact that it is finished and I can start on something else." She is particularly pleased with the red hibiscus.

The background is green overdyed with half Cushing's Reseda Green and half Black. Georgianne finished the rug with cording whipstitched with knitting wool dyed to match the background.

The Flying Hare, *52" x 37¹/₂", #8-cut wool on linen. Designed and hooked by Jan Gassner, Salem, Oregon, 1996.*

The Flying Hare
Third Place Readers' Choice—Original Design
Jan Gassner

The idea for Jan Gassner's rug grew out of her fascination with rabbits and her love of the view from the back window of her home, overlooking the Willamette Valley farmland and the Oregon coastal range. "One spring day," says Jan, "I placed a large piece of butcher paper on my kitchen counter, took out a box of pastels, and began to draw. Within a few hours, I had a detailed, life-sized, color drawing of what was to become my rug, *The Flying Hare.*" She transferred her drawing onto a piece of linen and began hooking like there was no tomorrow. "I was inspired! I finished the rug in a record 4¹/₂ months."

Jan used mostly recycled wool for the project, as she does for most of her rugs. She used as-is wool, plaids, and scraps from other projects to incorporate the colors of all four seasons into the landscape. She did dye some wool for special effects and for certain colors that she could not find in swatches. She dip dyed wool for the sky her favorite color of blue, and spot dyed the border with mahogany and navy blue.

The biggest challenge was hooking the landscape with wide-cut wool. Some areas had to be reworked a few times, and she hand-trimmed wool strips to fill some areas.

Jan finished the rug by folding the linen around polyester cording and whipstitching the edge with wool tapestry yarn. Then she trimmed the linen to about ³/₄" and hand sewed cotton binding tape to cover the cut edge.

"The rabbit is my favorite part of the rug. His size gives him a special importance—he is master of his domain. This project really tapped and stretched my imagination, and I am proud of the results because it's so... me."

Sunflowers
First Place Readers' Choice—Commercial Design
Gail Dufresne

When professional gardener Gail Dufresne saw this Jane McGown Flynn pattern, she described her reaction as love at first sight because it really captured the feel of these majestic flowers. Sunflowers are Gail's favorite flower, and at one of the estates where she works, every known variety of sunflower (including Gail's favorite—red) is grown along the fence that encloses the property.

"The most spectacular part of the sunflower border," Gail says, "is when the seeds have set in the fall and flocks of goldfinches swoop down to get their favorite treat. I try not to disturb them, but when I do have to walk by them, they all rush out in a gorgeous yellow flurry." So Patsy Becker drew a goldfinch into the pattern, then added a bee, her own business logo, and Gail's logo—a ladybug.

Barbara Miller, Gail's teacher at the Rugs by the Sea Camp in Cape May, New Jersey, was unconvinced that red sunflowers really did exist until she drove by a garden and saw one. She snapped a photo, and that photograph and a cover from *Fine Gardening* magazine inspired the color scheme of the rug. Gail used swatches for the red and yellow flowers, and Barbara dip dyed a combination of the two colors for the red sunflower. Gail used the same dip dye to hook a one-line separation between the outer border and the background.

Gail originally intended the background to be sky, but as she hooked, she discovered the background values were too similar to those of the sunflowers. So she took the wool Barbara had dyed for the sky, "threw tons of Cushing's Chartreuse and Navy over it, and mixed it with an as-is Pendleton plaid." That became the background wool. The border is a spot-dye formula, dyed over pink tweed. Gail finished the edges with the same wool as in the border.

Sunflowers, *30" x 54", #3- to 6-cut wool on burlap. Designed by Jane McGown Flynn; hooked by Gail Dufresne, Trenton, New Jersey, 1995.*

The Ladies, *29¹/₂" x 19¹/₂", #3- and 5-cut wool, cotton, and mohair on rug warp. Adapted from a poster and hooked by Carrie Jacobus, Oradell, New Jersey, 1996.*

The Ladies
Second Place Readers' Choice—Commercial Design
Carrie Jacobus

Carrie Jacobus really enjoyed working on this rug. "This was an unbelievable and fulfilling experience. I enjoyed every moment and didn't mind any of the work or running around. But I did have to deal with a postpartum depression phase when the ladies didn't need me anymore."

Carrie based her rug on a poster of five women in tight dresses whose backs revealed their varied body shapes. The poster made her laugh, and she decided that one day she would do her own interpretation of it. "The piece was originally titled *No Body's Perfect*," says Carrie, "but during its evolution everyone would ask how 'the ladies' were doing, so that name stuck."

Arline Bechtoldt helped Carrie decide on the transition colors that would give each dress shape and texture. Arline recommended Barbara Sleeper's transition dye formulas and helped Carrie determine that 6" of wool for each 1" of hooking would be necessary for a #3-cut rug. Carrie had already found the colors she wanted, so she matched them to Barbara's formulas, and she and Arline

dip dyed all day. Carrie used cotton rug warp for the backing because of its stiffness. She wanted to be sure that her stitches would hold their shape.

The hair for the ladies was a challenge. Carrie searched for the perfect mohair for each of them. "Originally, I had planned that all the women would have the same medium-brown shade," says Carrie, "but the Lady in Red kept calling me to make her a blonde. I didn't think it was right to penalize the others just because they weren't curvaceous, so I made sure they had their own colors."

For the background, she used a flat stitch, similar in look to the reverse stitch, but hooked from the front rather than the back. A regular hooking stitch was used for the border so that the border acts as a three-dimensional frame. Because of this three-dimensional aspect, Carrie didn't want to put the rug on the floor, so she sewed gray wool over the rug warp to hide it, then attached the rug to stretcher bars so that she could hang it.

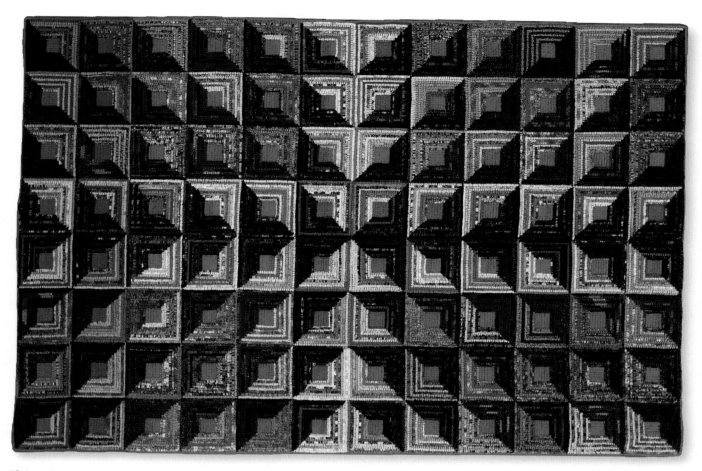

Flying Geese, *60" x 40", #5-cut wool on burlap. Adapted from quilt patterns and hooked by Charles Idler, Camp Hill, Pennsylvania, 1996.*

Flying Geese
Third Place Readers' Choice—Commercial Design
Charles Idler

Charles Idler uses two geometric patterns in his rug. The first is "flying geese," a variation of the log cabin quilt pattern. The flying geese design is made when sets of two triangles are joined to form larger right triangles, which are then placed point to back in a series. Black geese fly the length of the rug, and white geese fly the width. The second geometric pattern is known as straight furrows. This design is made when right triangles are placed sharp point to sharp point.

Coming up with just the right colors and combinations of squares for Flying Geese took plenty of planning. "I created the design by taking cardboard squares, drawing a diagonal line through each one, and coloring one half of each block," says Charles. "I played with these blocks until I happened across this surprise creation." Each square is about 5".

Charles planned the colors from "the mountain of wool in the basement." Although Charles enjoys dyeing wool for his projects, he found that he had all the colors he needed in his basement stack. He searched for just the right lights and darks that would produce the desired effect—a uniformity of tones that would not detract from the overall pattern.

"I like the way the eye keeps moving around the rug to see different patterns within the overall pattern," he says. "I wanted a traditional, geometric design that would keep the eye moving. The various lines and triangles within triangles achieve that. I confess, though, that the overall effect of this rug was a gift. It turned out far better than I could have hoped or imagined."

Charles finished *Flying Geese* as he does all of his rugs, by whipping the edges with a strong needlepoint yarn and then covering the raw edges of the backing with bias tape. While he has had no formal art training, he enjoys all of the processes that go into designing a new rug. "I love using color and form to create a thing of beauty," he says, "and that, after all, is what this is all about."

Celebration VIII—1998

Randolph Center 1945, *45" x 27", #4-cut wool on linen. Designed and hooked by Kate Smith, Oakland, California, 1997.*

WILLIAM M. BISHOP

Randolph Center 1945
First Place Readers' Choice—Original Design

Kate Smith

Kate Smith's strong memories of her home and siblings are the subject for this pictorial rug. With teacher Jane Olson's help, she illustrated her recollections and family photos in this original design.

Kate remembers moving her sister to the house across the street in a wheelbarrow, as seen in the rug, when her sister was seven and their family outgrew the home. "We had 600 laying hens in the barn, so Paul is gathering the eggs. Jean loves to read and was often off someplace quiet doing so. There are five stone walls on the property. This cat's name was Panther. Mother started her rosebush from Grandma's white rose. We had an apple orchard, so an apple tree was a must." The lilacs in the border represent the more than 130 bushes that still bloom there each spring.

"All four of us started school at the little red schoolhouse and worshiped in the white church (seen in the background of the rug). We were known to leave the house as either bell chimed and still get to church or school on time."

Roslyn Logsdon assisted Kate with the color plan. Kate dyed the wool for the lilacs and the border with jar, open pan, and scrunch dyeing. The rest of the rug was hooked with wool left over from other projects. "The hardest part was to get the right color to put behind the lilacs," Kate says.

It took Kate about six months to hook *Randolph Center 1945*. The rug is finished with yarn whipstitched over cording at the edges and twill tape sewn on the back.

The Rape of Europa, *39" x 36", hand-cut wool on rug warp. Designed and hooked by Jule Marie Smith, Ballston Spa, New York, 1997.*

The Rape of Europa
Second Place Readers' Choice—Original Design
Jule Marie Smith

Jule Marie Smith planned to exhibit *The Rape of Europa* at the 1995 Rugs of the Sea show at the Cahoon Museum on Cape Cod. The story of Europa, a Phoenician princess who was carried over the sea to Crete by Zeus disguised as a bull, is one that the retired English teacher didn't think anyone else would choose. But the sketches alone took a week, and the rug was not ready for the show. After exhibiting it as a piece in progress, Jule Marie put it away for two years, then finally completed what she describes as "the most difficult rug that I have ever drawn."

Borders are Jule Marie's specialty. The gods on Mount Olympus are looking at the scene from the top border. The clouds hint at eyes and faces; the profile of the woman looking away represents Hera, Zeus' wife, who knows exactly what her husband is up to but is pretending not to notice. The sides and bottom borders show

Poseidon and Triton, shells, seaweed, aquatic creatures and sea nymphs.

Many dyeing techniques, including spot, dip, drag, casserole, and open pot, went into creating *The Rape of Europa*. Jule Marie loves to use colors, contrasts, and multiple values of wools. "I had dyed baskets of interesting wools in the appropriate colors. I began with Europa, whose hair had purple highlights and whose dress was green. I placed her on a lovely, manly, rusty orange bull. I tried to capture the rush of the moment," Jule Marie says, "with tossed flowers and a lost shoe." Her biggest hurdle was how to add depth to the ocean. Jule Marie hooked waves on top for distance and used multiple dip dyes to make the water shimmer.

The Rape of Europa was Jule Marie's second rug with a mythological theme. "[Who knows] what possibilities lie ahead," she muses.

Our Captain Stood, *47" x 40', #6-cut wool on burlap. Designed and hooked by Pris Butler, Gainsville, Georgia, 1997.*

Our Captain Stood
Third Place Readers' Choice—Original Design
Pris Butler

Pris Butler, a full-time painter of American primitives, began rug hooking in the summer of 1996 at the Blue Ridge Rug Camp where Marianne Storm offered her advice and materials. "Marianne showed me how to use plaids for the sailors' shirts and suggested creating an inner border of green plaid and outlining the letters with the same wool. When I got home I didn't have enough of her green, so I started dyeing to see if I could get the same shade.

"Since I am a painter and mix colors all the time, blending the dyes particularly fascinated me," she says. But she discovered that dyeing fabric and mixing paint were entirely different, and she recalls "many failures along the way" as she experimented.

Pris began with the bear and then worked on the harpoon boat

and whales. For the churning water, she used blues left over from a previous rug and tried to mix them as harmoniously as possible. She consciously strove for a cold look, especially in the bear, the icebergs, and the ship's sails.

Selecting and combining the right whites from new and recycled fabric was the most challenging aspect of the rug. She is interested in the Grenfell style of hooking in horizontal rows, and applied this technique to the sky, using subtle shades of blue.

Pris considers rug hooking a good way to unwind at day's end. "It's relaxing, and the rugs are wonderful to behold when finished," she says.

Dutch Treat, *37" x 28", #3-cut wool on burlap. Designed by Gretchen Leiberg; hooked by Mary Arrington, Marysville, Washington, 1997.*

Dutch Treat
First Place Readers' Choice—Commercial Design
Mary Arrington

Although Mary Arrington usually designs or adapts patterns, she uses commercial patterns when she finds one she likes. *Dutch Treat* was designed by Northwest artist Gretchen Leiberg in 1979. Gretchen drew her designs freehand directly on backing, so no two patterns are exactly alike. "She designed as I wish I could," says Mary, "and those of us who have her designs really treasure them."

Mary began work on *Dutch Treat* in 1980, but when she and her husband moved to Alaska for four years, *Dutch Treat* went into storage. When she next attended a rug camp she took the rug with her, and Kay Oldford taught her "the technique of generalization instead of exact detail in pictorials," she says. Mary worked on the rug over the years, but did not finish it until after her husband's death in 1996. "It was my greatest therapy during a very hard time in my life."

Mary says she can't believe her own farsightedness in collecting, sorting, and most important, organizing all the blue and almost-blue wool right from the start. All the material for this Delft-inspired piece became a specific part of the scene—a tree, water, cloud, building, and so on—which she had labeled and packaged accordingly. Almost all the fabrics were recycled solid wools or plaids and checks. Mary also used a couple of commercial swatches in the border and an Imari blue piece she had dyed for another rug project.

She drew her inspiration for the clouds partly by trial and error and partly by observation. "The clouds needed to be dramatic enough to balance the design without becoming dark and stormy and changing the color balance." The buildings came easily for Mary since, she explains, structures are frequently the subjects of her drawings.

Cats
Second Place Readers' Choice—Commercial Design
Sibyl Osicka

Sibyl Osicka knew she was on the right track when two of her real felines started to hiss at the new cats in the house—the hooked ones. "When that happened," Sibyl says, "I knew I had achieved in my hooking what I had wanted to do."

Cats was drawn on rug warp by Elizabeth Black. Sibyl then used photographs of each cat to plan the colors and dye new wool from the Dorr Woolen Mills to match their fur. "The two top cats were the hardest to hook because of their coloring," Sibyl says. "The seal point cat is almost black, but I used many different colors to give the effect of black. If I had used only black wool it would have looked flat."

Sibyl dip dyed the background to get just the right colors. She needed depth at the base of the background to balance the wall hanging. Sibyl used swatches but selected only the values needed to make the fur realistic. And she used some spot-dyed wool and some dark gray right off the bolt.

To finish the piece, Sibyl cut a piece of wool a little larger than the hooked portion, laid it in on the front of the rug, and stitched the two pieces together on three sides, leaving an opening at the top. She turned the pocket inside out (the hooked portion was now on the outside), pressed it, and made a sleeve at the top to hold a rod.

Cats, *17" x 60", #3-cut wool on rug warp. Designed by Elizabeth Black; hooked by Sibyl Osicka, Parma, Ohio, 1997.*

November, *17" x 60", #3- and 4-cut wool on burlap. Designed by Jane McGown Flynn; hooked by Betty Conley, Berea, Ohio, 1997.*

November
Third Place Readers' Choice—Commercial Design
Betty Conley

Of all the things she's hooked—from geometrics, fruits and vegetables, scrolls, stained glass, and American Indian designs—Betty Conley particularly likes to hook leaves. After admiring Jane McGown Flynn's leaf-filled *November* at a teacher's workshop, Betty decided to present it at the workshop the following year.

Preparing her own color plan, she used mostly new wool manipulated with various dyeing techniques: "I used onion skins to dye over yellow and corn wool for the big basswood leaves; Transcolor and casserole dyeing for the maples, oaks, cherry, and dogwood; dip dyeing for the elm; and casserole dyeing over several different colored wools for the woodbine leaves." She overdyed tweeds for acorn caps and used casserole-dyed recycled fabric in some small

leaves. By using a single dye formula learned from Orpha Blaisdell and dyeing it in varying strengths over different colors of wool, she created a great variety of oak leaves.

Betty loves autumn in all its glory, but it took real planning to make each leaf in her rug look different. She hooked strips as they came out of the cutter, thus controlling where the colors appeared. When the rug was completed, she whipstitched its edges with wool tapestry yarn and covered the raw edges of the backing with twill tape.

November won a best in class award a local fair, and it was exhibited at the Southern Teachers Workshop and at a northeastern Ohio exhibation.

Celebration IX—1999

Inside the Ark, *60" x 36", #2- and #3-cut wool on rug warp. Designed and hooked by Elizabeth Black, Bentonville, Virginia, 1998.* IMPACT XPOZURES

Inside the Ark
First Place Readers' Choice—
Original Design
Elizabeth Black

Inside the Ark, a novel viewpoint of an old story, was commissioned by Dale and Marny Cardin of San Luis Obispo, California. "I wanted to design something a little different," Elizabeth says, "and decided to do a scene from inside the ark."

Elizabeth was limited in the size and shapes of animals she could select by the rug's 3' x 5' dimensions. She confronted two challenges: The first was selecting a mix of animals that gave the design the proper outline and flow. She drew a variety of animals on paper and moved them around, experimenting with different combinations of shapes and positions until she achieved a satisfying balance. The second test was harmonizing the colors of the creatures.

Friend and fellow fiber artist Maxine Gallagher supplied spot-, dip-, and casserole-dyed new wool to achieve just the right blends for this menagerie. This wool supplemented new wool from Elizabeth's own supply, which she purchases whenever and wherever she finds something appealing. Most of *Inside the Ark* was done in a #3 cut, but she notes that the shading and detail in some of the animals' heads could only be achieved with a #2 cut. To finish her rug, Elizabeth machine-sewed rug binding tape to the edges of the backing. She then turned it under and hand stitched it down.

This intricate project took six months to complete, and the owners were delighted with the finished rug. Elizabeth finds the most enjoyment "from designing a rug and then seeing it take on form and a personality through color…. I continually look for new ideas in design and color that will stretch my imagination and talent."

Spring, *29" x 22", #3-cut wool on burlap. Designed and hooked by Mollie E. McBride, Houston, Texas, 1998.* IMPACT XPOZURES

Spring
Second Place Readers' Choice—Original Design
Mollie E. McBride

Mollie McBride has slowly been turning her traditional paintings into wool paintings. *Spring* is just such a work, inspired by a watercolor Mollie painted in her Nova Scotia backyard. "It was early May; the first color of spring was emerging. The trees were just beginning to bud, giving rise to muted shades of taupe and subtle browns, rust, grays, and yellow-greens. The day was gray with a Scotch mist. I decided to try to capture this mood in a hooking."

It took Mollie about a month to dye her basic palette, and she found herself returning to the dyeing process as she searched for a wider range of color. Experimenting with Cushing dyes over unbleached Dorr wool, Mollie started with pan dyeing to get her basic hues, then switched to casserole and spot dyeing, with some over dyeing as necessary. The paler shades of yellow and taupe were jar dyed. Mollie says she used as little water as possible to obtain nicely variegated swatches.

"The most challenging aspect was the dyeing," she says. "I found it difficult to produce the delicate hues of rose, rust, and taupe shades I needed. I used variations of mulberry, cherry, dark green, khaki, and taupe, sometimes with a little rust. I mixed blues and yellows to provide the greens…. And the large areas of off-white were difficult to keep very light yet colorful enough to provide a three-dimensional effect."

Mollie took a novel approach to the actual hooking: she started at the upper left corner of the pattern and worked her way down and across the burlap, using whatever color seemed appropriate. She took her time with the project. "I often left problem areas until solutions came to mind." She tried to avoid preconceived notions about the final appearance of *Spring*, observing that "unexpected results often lead to new directions that are more interesting than the original concept."

Prize Catch, *34" x 22", #3-cut wool on monk's cloth. Designed and hooked by Darlene Bryan, Columbia, Missouri, 1998.* IMPACT XPOZURES

Prize Catch
Third Place Readers' Choice—Original Design
Darlene Bryan

When your son is a professional wildlife photographer who loves fly fishing, you can't go wrong with an outdoors theme for a hooked rug for his home. This holiday gift was a labor of love as well as a challenge, requiring several new techniques and tricks from its artist.

Retired from the banking industry and an antiques business, Darlene Bryan found new horizons in two art forms, painting and rug hooking. So serious is she about painting that she has gone on watercolor holidays to France and England. So it was natural for her to first create a watercolor of a trout to use as a design aid while planning the rug's colors. Doing this was the best way, she says, to keep in mind the subtle shadings of the real fish. That shading was the fun part of hooking *Prize Catch*.

The test in hooking this rug came while creating the lively plaid border. "It was a new experience for me. I tried to work in all the colors that are in the trout." Darlene felt a plaid border would

be a nice, masculine setting for this subject. She was inspired to try it from an article on creative stitchery she had seen in *Rug Hooking* magazine.

Darlene likes to work with recycled wools, looking in local thrift shops for different shades of white and other pale hues that might take dye well. "I have quite a collection of 'antique' Rit dyes. Some of them must be 50 years old! But I just get them out and work with what I have." *Prize Catch* was all done in recycled wool, most of which was dip dyed by Darlene, while the rest was used as is.

She finished the outer edge with cording, which she overcast with tapestry yarn. She then applied rug tape to cover the turned-under edge of the backing. She presented the finished rug to her wildlife photographer/fly fisherman son who was thrilled with a present that included a hooked version of his flies, his fishing rod and reel, and a prize catch.

Currier & Ives' Wintertime: A Stop at the Inn, *40" x 26", #3-cut wool on burlap. Designed by Pearl K. McGown; hooked by Mildred Prall, Fort Myers, Florida, 1998.* IMPACT XPOZURES

Currier & Ives' Wintertime: A Stop at the Inn
First Place Readers' Choice—Commercial Design
Mildred Prall

Good things take time. And that was certainly the case with *Currier & Ives' Wintertime: A Stop at the Inn*. This Pearl McGown pattern caught Mildred Prall's eye at the McGown Northern Teachers Workshop in Massachusetts in the early 1970s, but she didn't finish it until nearly 25 years later.

Mildred planned the colors based on the original illustration, which was drawn for a calendar. She dyed most of the wool, using gradation, spot, casserole, and painted methods. Some wool used for the sky and ice was purchased from Alice Persons, who had taught the pattern at the workshop.

Over a period of years she added more loops to the pattern as she came across suitable pieces. Eventually, the right half of the rug was finished. But it wasn't until her husband requested that it be completed for his room that she seriously committed to finishing the piece.

Hooking the legs of the horses tested Mildred's skill, although she has 52 years of rug making under her hook. "It was a problem

to make a loop or get an end to pull through so that it looked enough like a leg." The rocky area behind the inn was also troublesome. "But setting in the loops of the sky with those magnificent colors was pure joy."

Horse & Buggy Days, *36" x 26", #3-cut wool on burlap. Designed by Louise Hunter Zeiser; hooked by Shirley Lyons, Georgetown, Ontario, Canada, 1998.* CATHERINE TURNER

Horse & Buggy Days
Second Place Readers' Choice—Commercial Design
Shirley Lyons

Shirley began this rug in the early 1970s, while attending a workshop on pictorials taught by Jeanne Field. "We were all new to this type of hooking," she says, "and my choice of pattern was overwhelming for a novice. I worked on the tree trunk with a variety of textures and realized that tree bark has more colors than brown."

Shirley chose this design from an Heirloom rug catalog because it rekindled memories of her great-grandfather, who had been a carriage maker and the proprietor of Miller Carriage Works in Attercliffe, Ontario. The tree reminded her of the horse chestnut trees near her childhood home, and the horse evoked memories of Joe, a dapple-gray she owned as a young girl.

When she had hooked about a third of the rug, Shirley suffered a back injury that prevented her from sitting for long periods of time and forced her to put the project aside for many years. She continued to attend lectures and workshops pertaining to pictori-

als, however, and dyed much of the wool she would need to complete *Horse & Buggy Days.*

A spot-dye, graded swatch gave the barn a weathered look, and the buggy and horse were hooked with a swatch dyed from black to white. She hooked the road with a variety of spot dyes in grays and browns and taupe. To hook the tree she knew she would need many shades of yellow and blue-green for perspective; she used 15 different greens to achieve the depth she wanted.

Shirley vowed to have her rug completed in time for the thirtieth anniversary of the Georgetown guild, in 1998. With only five weeks left, she was stalled again when she discovered the rug's burlap had become brittle after having been stored so long, and she needed to mend it. Her work progressed smoothly after she made the necessary repairs.

When the rug was completed, Shirley had it professionally framed.

Winston, *15" x 15", #3-cut wool on rug warp. Designed by Elizabeth Black; hooked by Sandra L. Brown, Pittsburgh, Pennsylvania, 1997.* IMPACT XPOZURES

Winston
Third Place Readers' Choice—Commercial Design
Sandra L. Brown

To master highlighting techniques, Sandra Brown studied with Elizabeth Black. When Elizabeth suggested hooking a character dog, Sandra enthusiastically agreed. Elizabeth sketched the dog, dubbed Winston by her class, onto a piece of rug warp for Sandy, who says she then naively dyed "all the wrong values of wool" for the next class. Fortunately, she was able to purchase better colors from her classmates. The key, she learned, is gradation swatches so subtle in their gradients that the shading takes care of itself.

Sandy knew that choosing a natural subject would limit her palette. The biggest hurdle for her was shading all of Winston's wrinkles and folds, because so many of them are the same basic color. She needed spot-dyed wool as well as some recycled tweeds

to add texture as she strove for realistic distinctions between Winston's face and body. Such a regally named creature demanded a suitable background, so she picked hues of royal purple mixed with black.

Working on *Winston* put Sandy in an unusual state of mind. She says that with exactly the right materials and some good direction, for which she freely and heartily thanks Elizabeth, "it is possible to get into a 'zone' when hooking. You can almost do no wrong."

Sandy fell in love with Winston's sweet expression and decided to make her creation into a pillow so she could see his face every day. She finished it with a braided cord edge and the pillow earned a place of honor on a rocking chair in her living room.

The Brothers, *21" x 16", #2- to 4-cut wool and wool blends on Verel. Designed and hooked by Louise Koger, Vestal, New York, 1997.* IMPACT XPOZURES

The Brothers
Third Place Readers' Choice—Original Design
Louise Koger

*T*he Brothers by Louise Koger was inspired by a cherished childhood photograph of her husband and his brother. The boys grew up on an Indiana farm where "there were always plenty of barn cats for them to play with."

She used a tinted 8" x 10" enlargement of the original black-and-white snapshot as reference. After placing outlines of the major elements and enlarging the pattern to the correct size, Louise added details freehand, then used a light box to transfer the finished pattern onto Verel.

It required patience to put in the fine details. "It was important to my husband that their mother's shoes, left out on the porch, were visible." She made sure the boys and cats were squinting in the bright sunshine. She found that shadows are difficult to create

with wool. "They were the most challenging aspect, as were the boys' and the cats' faces, because they were so small. The secret…to the shadows was to find the right color." By the end of the four months it took her to complete the piece, she actually enjoyed hooking shadows.

Basing her color plan on the hues of the tinted enlargement tested Louise's abilities. With Nancy MacLennan's advice, she carefully selected most of the wool from her own supply, supplementing it with a texture she dyed in light, medium, and dark values for the boys' overalls. Louise wanted the background dull (to make the subjects stand out) and simple (so the viewer's eyes are not distracted).

The Brothers was professionally framed.

Celebration X—2000

Young Girl With Kitten
First Place Readers' Choice—Original Design
Victoria Hart Ingalls

Victoria Hart is fascinated by the techniques used by late nineteenth-century watercolor portraitists. *Young Girl With Kitten* was inspired by one of these portraits, which Victoria translated beautifully into what she calls "a painting in wool, with lots of the fine shading that I love."

Victoria, who dyes much of her own wool, planned the colors and dyed the background in three closely graduated shades. The colors for the face were swatches from Connie Charleson, and other areas were hooked with swatches from Jane Olson. Victoria used both new and recycled wool in this piece.

The portrait provided many opportunities to use her favorite shading techniques, especially on the girl's sleeve and shoulder. "It took me more than 10 hours one day to complete just this portion. I laid out all my pastel swatches, along with my scrap bag, and began to experiment. There was a lot of putting in and pulling out loops." In contrast, Victoria says she "enjoyed most

doing the faces of the girl and the kitten."

Finishing *Young Girl With Kitten* took several steps. First, Victoria placed a double row of machine stitching beyond the edge of the hooking, then she trimmed the excess backing. Next, her husband cut a piece of foam core to the same size as the hooking, and Victoria cut and glued a slightly smaller piece of quilt batting to one side of it. She then placed the hooked rug face down, positioned the foam core (batting side down) on top of it, and glued the edges of the monk's cloth around the back of the core. After it dried, Victoria placed the piece in an antique white frame and hung it next to a Victorian dollhouse.

Young Girl with Kitten, *17" x 21", #3-cut wool on monk's cloth. Designed and hooked by Victoria Hart Ingalls, Independence, Missouri, 1999.* IMPACT XPOZURES

Market at Mahone Bay, *29" x 37", #3-cut wool on wool kimonos. Designed and hooked by Fumiyo Hachisuka, Tokyo, Japan, 1999.* IMPACT XPOZURES

Market at Mahone Bay
Second Place Readers' Choice—Original Design
Fumiyo Hachisuka

Fumiyo Hachisuka was so moved by brilliant orange pumpkins lining a stand at the Mahone Bay Market in Nova Scotia that she decided to capture the moment in wool. A few sketches later, *Market at Mahone Bay* was ready to hook.

For this rug, Fumiyo dyed natural wool with Cushing's Orange and Reseda Green. She dyed swatches using combinations of Orange, Crimson, and Bright Green; and Reseda Green, Buttercup, and Chartreuse. The turquoise-green sky was dip dyed—a technique Fumiyo says she most often uses for scenery.

Fumiyo's training as a painter was invaluable for this project when she needed to alter sections of the scene. Because the inside of the store was very dark, she couldn't see the goods inside clearly, so she changed the image and hooked many apples and pumpkins. Adding the produce and keeping it in perspective took planning. In the background, she used smaller shapes and weaker contrasts to produce the effect of distance. "I learned that I can have as much fun hooking a rug as I do painting in oils."

Fumiyo added scarecrows and the woman shopper to the picture. She struggled to get the woman's skirt just right. Fumiyo's favorite parts of the rug are the pumpkins in the cart and on the roof—they speak of autumn and the harvest.

Courting, *38" x 51", #3- to 5-cut wool on linen. Designed and hooked by Susan Quicksall, Oglesby, Texas, 1999.* IMPACT XPOZURES

Courting
Third Place Readers' Choice—Original Design
Susan Quicksall

Susan Quicksall loves needlepoint samplers made by young girls in the eighteenth and nineteenth centuries. Based on Early American stitched samplers, *Courting* uses many of Susan's favorite sampler elements. In fact, it is a companion piece to one of her own needlepoint samplers.

Courting was hooked with all wool flannel, mostly Dorr's natural and white, which Susan dyed to achieve her palette. She determined the rug's colors as she worked. "I really did not have a color plan," she says, "but started with the yellow house and chose colors as I progressed, knowing that I would eventually end with an as-is black background for the border." Color samples from when she was teaching herself how to dye worked in nicely as the rug took

shape. "Because I had all of my learning swatches, spots, and dips, I was able to pick and choose just the right color and shade. Some of my dyeing mistakes proved to be some of my favorite colors."

Susan kept a detailed dyeing journal to track the large number of colors and shades she used, 192 colors in all. She says it was difficult to maintain the simplicity of an Early American sampler while using such a range of colors.

"I hooked the raccoon with my two-year-old grandson, Alex, sitting on my lap attentively watching each loop being pulled up as the raccoon took shape. When he visits he goes to see his raccoon on the rug. It's a great memory."

Le Chateau, *25" x 19", #3-cut wool on cotton. Designed by Jane McGown Flynn; hooked by Eric H. Sandberg, West Toluca Lake, California, 1999.* IMPACT XPOZURES

Le Chateau
First Place Readers' Choice—Commercial Design
Eric H. Sandberg

Eric Sandberg was almost ready to give up on the idea of hooking *Le Chateau*. But he found that simply turning it upside down was all he had to do to convince himself that he could complete this pictorial. Remembering how well he fared during an art exercise of copying a line drawing of a man, Eric decided to use that same technique here. "The trick of the exercise was to turn the drawing upside down and then draw the lines. Somehow in the act of drawing upside down the brain is confused and doesn't know it's drawing a man. It just draws what it sees as lines on the paper. When the drawing is turned right side up, it's amazing how good it is."

Eric's rug hooking teacher, Jane Olson, suggested that Eric work on *Le Chateau* by hooking one section at a time, but this approach bothered him. He didn't see how he could isolate different elements and still integrate them into the overall picture.

So he decided to cover up the entire pattern except for a small window exposing what he was hooking. He did the same with his visual aid, so that its window corresponded to the window on the pattern. Recalling the drawing exercise, he turned both the rug and the visual aid upside down and just hooked what he saw. "By not hooking a tree, I hooked highlights and shadows," Eric explains, and by not hooking leaves, he hooked "light, medium, and dark greens instead."

When he was finished hooking the individual sections, Eric turned *Le Chateau* right side up. To his astonishment, the technique had worked and the piece was surprisingly good. "I'm amazed how it turned out," he says.

Eric's scene is full of color. He dyed no wool for the project—all the material was left over from previous projects.

Looking Out to Sea, *19" x 26", #3-cut wool on burlap. Adapted from a Norman Rockwell painting and hooked by Anne Howell, Beltsville, Maryland, 1998.* IMPACT XPOZURES

Looking Out to Sea
Second Place Readers' Choice—Commercial Design
Anne Howell

Anne Howell and her mother, Bernice, had amassed a huge collection of recycled wool when Anne decided to hook *Looking Out to Sea*. "I think my mother was as excited as I was to find the perfect pieces," Anne says. "It was wonderful to have such an assortment to choose from—plaids, tweeds, spot dyes—I didn't need to dye anything."

The project was much more complex than her earlier projects. But she put aside her self-confessed perfectionist tendencies and decided to have fun.

Anne hooked the dog first. "Much to my delight, in one attempt he turned out just the way I wanted." The craggy rocks and fluffy clouds were a challenge. Anne tried bright white wools to depict fluffy clouds in a sunny sky, but they looked gray and gloomy so she used a creamy white instead.

Anne says that with this project she learned to trust her own instincts and try different things. "Who knows? It may just work the first time. But if it doesn't, the nice thing about rug hooking is that you can always take loops out and try something different."

Carousel Horse, *37³/4" x 28", #3-cut wool on rug warp. Designed by Jane McGown Flynn; hooked by Sibyl Osicka, Parma, Ohio, 1999.* IMPACT XPOZURES

Carousel Horse
Third Place Readers' Choice—Commercial Design
Sibyl Osicka

As most veteran rug hookers do, Sibyl Osicka welcomed the opportunity to learn new techniques. "I had never hooked a horse before, so I learned where all the muscles are. And I had never hooked armor before… and I discovered that it was so much fun to hook." Her love of Victoriana originally led her to rug hooking, so it's little wonder that carousel steeds, ornate expressions of the woodcarvers' art, appeal to her.

Sibyl used all new Dorr wool in *Carousel Horse*. She envisioned an almost-black horse draped with velvet fabric over its brass and copper armor. For added interest, Sibyl made the fabric near the horse's tail appear to be threaded through a brass ring, adding even more dimension.

For the proud stallion's lustrous coat, Sibyl used an 8-value swatch dyed with PRO Chem black. An 8-value red swatch,

shaded from brilliant crimson to dark red, was perfect for the velvet drapery. The copper and brass of the armor are made of 8-value swatches. Sibyl dip dyed the red background with the same black as the horse to tie all the colors together. "By hooking the background in a sunburst fashion, the horse became the focal point." She also used the horse formula to dip dye the picket fence in the border, further unifying the piece. "I hooked the outer border to represent a picture frame, placing the highlight in the center and the darker values at the edges." The striking blacks and reds produced the dramatic, eye-catching look Sibyl was after.

Sibyl finished *Carousel Horse* by lining it with black fabric, and she added a sleeve for hanging. Her husband made a rod and end pieces. "This is truly a fantasy piece," says Sibyl, "and we all need fantasy pieces at one time or another."

Celebration XI—2001

248 Outlook Drive
First Place Readers' Choice—
Commercial Design

Sandra Brown

The colors we see at dusk, dawn, and in moonlight, have long fascinated Sandra Brown. So when Sandra knew that she and her family would be moving away from 248 Outlook Drive, she decided to create a pictorial rug depicting one of her favorite views of their beloved home: this moonlit scene that she often admired when walking the dog.

A former lighting designer, Sandra explains that the colors we see are completely dependent upon the type of light that illuminates them. Accurately portraying in the same project the cool natural shades of the moonlight and the warm yellow hues of the porch light would be demanding. The challenges for her as a rug hooker were how to depict those colors in wool and how to dye them.

No single dyeing method would give Sandra the palette she needed, so she used a variety of techniques, including dip dyeing for the moon and clouds and swatch and open pan dyeing for the trees, lawn, and porch light. "Textures are a basic component of pictorials," she says, and in this pictorial they formed the bricks, roof, and other elements. New wool dyed in swatches and dip dyed in large batches was used for the smooth, unbroken areas, such as the sky, land, and sidewalk. Dip dyeing over white wool gave Sandra the perfect moonlight effect. "The sky was the most challenging aspect of the rug since there's so much of it. I kept running out of wool… and needing to re-dye it. The moon and clouds were my favorite parts." And, she notes with justifiable pride, "I only had to hook that area once."

Sandra had *248 Outlook Drive* professionally framed. "My youngest son has put his dibs on this rug for a future office, since this house is where he grew up."

248 Outlook Drive, *40" x 29", #3-cut wool on burlap. Designed and hooked by Sandra Brown, Pittsburgh, Pennsylvania, 2000.* DAVID ALBRECHT

Too Close to Call, *48" x 30", #7-cut wool and yarn on linen. Designed and hooked by Abby Vakay, Alexandria, Virginia, 2000.* SCOTT FINGER/IMPACT XPOZURES

Too Close Too Call
Second Place Readers' Choice—Original Design
Abby Vakay

After completing a highly detailed fine-cut pictorial of a steeplechase race, Abby Vakay was looking for a new challenge. As a life-long horsewoman, horses are one of her favorite topics, so *Too Close to Call* was a natural for her.

She wanted to hook a rug with a wider cut of wool and a simpler design than earlier works. "My idea was to hook the last few exciting seconds of a flat race with 'in your face' action." She wanted to portray the slinging mud, sweaty horses, and the intensity of the jockeys. She wanted the picture to be blurry, as if the rug were a photo of the race. Her strategy was to hook a tight and detailed foreground with only the suggestion of a background. "I can say I learned new concepts and saw them come together for a successful and satisfying end result," she said.

Abby hooked the horses in unusual colors, such as blues and purples; she carefully chose the hues that would appear as browns and grays once they were hooked into the rug. "As I began hooking, each strip I used was a different color from the one before. This really kept me on my toes!" Known for her use of unusual materials, *Too Close to Call* is no exception. "I used many types of yarn, both thick and thin, and most were overdyed," she said. "I especially enjoyed pulling up fuzzy yarns to show the mud, the saddle pads, the muzzles, and the bridles."

For Abby, the action is the best part of the scene. "You can almost feel the pounding hooves. . .You can tell it's the final seconds of the race by the various stances of the jockeys with their whips flying. . . Who's winning? We don't know. That's what makes it exciting!"

Shadows on Snow, *19" x 26", #3- and #4-cut wool and acrylic/wool yarn on linen. Designed and hooked by Bernice Howell, Beltsville, Maryland, 2000.* SCOTT FINGER/IMPACT XPOZURES

Shadows on Snow
Third Place Readers' Choice—Original Design
Bernice Howell

Bernice Howell and her husband awoke one morning to find that it had snowed, and they were awestruck by the backyard's beauty. Bernice wanted to preserve the scene—in full color with the pure white of the fresh snow against the azure blue sky. But the photos she took for her design reminded Bernice of an Ansel Adams print instead. So she decided to hook the snow, shed, and trees in stark, simple, black and white.

She learned an important technique about hooking snow: "Do white last!" she says. If the brightest whites are hooked first, they pick up so much lint from the other colors that they become dull. "I had to re-hook fresh snow on the lower tree branches because

the snow had picked up a lot of gray lint, dulling the contrast between it and the lighter sky near the horizon." And some of her seemingly perfect white strips looked dirty when she hooked them into the large areas of snow-covered ground. They too had picked up lint from rubbing against other colors in the box, so she needed more white wool. She used a skein of white acrylic/wool yarn given to her by a friend.

The background trees and shrubs took some trial and error to work out. By the time Bernice got to the white oak tree, she truly enjoyed hooking it. This tree is like a dear old friend, "a treasured part of our backyard."

King Henry VIII, *30¹/₂" x 44", #3-cut wool on rug warp. Adapted from Hans Holbein's painting and hooked by Lorraine Williams, Bernardsville, New Jersey, 2000.* SCOTT FINGER/IMPACT XPOZURES

King Henry VIII
First Place Readers' Choice—Commercial Design
Lorraine Williams

The inspiration for Lorraine Williams's project comes from the works of German Renaissance painter, Hans Holbein the Younger. She saw his portrait of King Henry VIII on a visit to the Morgan Library in New York City; she couldn't get it out of her mind and decided to put a hooker's spin on this unusual subject.

Betty McClentic, a rug hooking teacher to whom Lorraine turned for help, agreed to draw the image on rug warp and plan the colors. Lorraine had experience dyeing wool, but she knew that many different techniques and lots of time would be required to reproduce the luminous quality of Holbein's painting. So Lorraine

left the dyeing to her teacher.

Bringing *King Henry VIII* to life in wool was much more difficult than Lorraine ever dreamed it would be. "Getting… the shadows just so made it strenuous and interesting." Highlights and shadows, she points out, are what make the piece distinctive. The constanly changing patterns of Henry's regal raiment, the background tapestry, and the intricately patterned Oriental rug were particularly difficult. But it was easy to identify her favorite part— Henry's face. "Imperious, intelligent, and haughty. And did I ever learn a thing or two about hooking a face while I did it!"

In Grandmother's Garden, *13¹/₂" x 20", #3-cut wool and beads on Scottish burlap. Adapted from Marie-Francois Firmin-Girard's painting and hooked by Susan Elcox, Garden Valley, Idaho, 2000.* MEDIA SPECIALTIES, BOISE, IDAHO

In Grandmother's Garden
Second Place Readers' Choice—Commercial Design

Susan Elcox

A painting by Marie-Francois Firmin-Girard led Susan Elcox to create this adaptation. Susan loved the women's clothing and the autumnal background. The original painting contained three figures; Susan wanted to learn to hook faces, but she felt that two were enough for her first attempt, so she omitted one figure when she drew the pattern.

Joan Reckwardt dyed the wool for the rug. She suggested using sculpturing techniques and some special stitches to achieve the illusion of depth that Susan wanted to capture.

Susan wanted her hooking to flow freely in the background and didn't particularly care if it was exact to the painting. She supple-

mented the spot dyes Joan had provided with eight to ten other dyes. Emphasizing oranges, browns, greens, and blues, Susan brought the feel of a fall day to the hooking. She hooked the leaves on the trees in the foreground higher than the rest of the background to add dimension.

Susan was pleased with the results, especially the woman's black dress. ". . . the folds turned out very well. I also very much love the background, the sky, and the leaves in the trees." She added beads to make a comb in the hair of the woman in black, and beads at the base of the cap of the woman in purple.

My Jane, *36" x 25", #3-cut wool on monk's cloth. Designed by Julie Luedtke; hooked by Jean Johnson, Grand Blanc, Michigan, 2000.*
SCOTT FINGER/IMPACT XPOZURES

My Jane
Third Place Readers' Choice—Commercial Design
Jean Johnson

Jean Johnson met Cynthia Hanson while Cynthia was working on a portrait of a dog. Jean loved the design and was inspired to do a dog rug of her own. She asked the rug's designer, Julie Luedtke, to create a portrait of Jane, her daughter's Jack Russell terrier.

Julie and Cynthia, partners in the Rug Thyme Studio, used dip, spot, and jar dyes on new wool for the rug. The dyeing included a dozen shades of red for the bricks. "The spot dye they did for the grout was fantastic," Jean said.

Jean's teacher, Victoria Hart Ingalls, helped to bring *My Jane* to life. Portrait pieces are usually hooked face first, so Jane's attentive canine countenance kept Jean company throughout the process. But it was the dog's body that was the real hurdle. Since Jane is mostly white, Jean had to work with many different values of gray and white. This wasn't easy for someone so comfortable with primitive techniques. "If it hadn't been for Victoria's support and direction this would never have come alive the way it did."

Jean finished the rug by whipping the edges, changing the wools to match the colors at the rug's edge and combining different hues to blend with the mottled colors of the flowers and bricks.

Celebration XII—2002

Fantasy Floral

First Place Readers' Choice—Original Design
Michelle Lechleiter

At a staggering 12'1" x 9'8", *Fantasy Floral* is truly Michelle Lechleiter's hand-hooked masterpiece. A rug hooker since 1991, Michelle devoted more than half of her hooking career to this whimsical work. Started in 1995, *Fantasy Floral* was finally completed in 2001.

Perhaps because she worked on it so long, Michelle Lechleiter finds it hard to pick a favorite part, but she narrowed it down to three. She loves the colors she selected to hook the romping bugs. She is also fond of the handprints of her family members, including her grandmother's who died in 2001 at age 101. And the birds and birdhouses in the design that her children drew when young are especially dear to her now that they are teenagers.

Describing the most difficult part of her 12'1" x 9'8" rug, however, was much easier for Michelle—"its weight and size toward the end. It felt like dragging dead weight around."

The articles she read about large projects reinforced Michelle's inclination to plan for the difficulties involved in hooking massive rug, not easy for Michelle who prefers the "draw, hook, and evolve" method of planning a project.

"I have no confidence in my drawing ability, so I created 'fantasy' flowers so I couldn't make a mistake," Michelle explains. "The traditional corner pineapples became birdhouses. I love personalizing my work, which led to the family handprints in the background. And the bug border was pure whimsy."

For practical and economic reasons, Michelle planned to use as much found wool as possible. She chose navy blue for the background because it was a color she could find easily on thrift-store expeditions. She had to do some spot and paintbrush dyeing for special colors, but almost all of the materials were used as is.

Fantasy Floral, *12'1" x 9'8", #6-cut wool on linen. Designed and hooked by Michelle Lechleiter, Lusby, Maryland, 2001.* IMPACT XPOZURES

Rabbit Hill
Second Place Readers' Choice—
Original Design
Susan Quicksall

While hooking *Rabbit Hill*, Susan learned something unexpected: "No matter how ugly a piece of wool is, it can be used someday." But Susan's most important lesson was this: "Avoid hooking large areas horizontally (as in lawn and sky), then placing large vertical areas (as in borders) perpendicular to them. Vertical rows stretch less than horizontal rows."

Rabbit Hill transports viewers to summer at their home in the foothills of the Texas Hill Country. She incorporated favorite memories—family pets; local flora and fauna; pecan trees and roses in their garden; and the big hill out back, home to multitudes of rabbits, coyotes, and even a cougar.

Susan kept the background colors subtle and the background elements small to suggest distance; the foreground is brighter and clearer, and the subjects there are larger to draw the viewer into the scene. She used many different dye sources—Triple Over Dyes, Carroll and Lais' *Antique Colours*, and spot dyes by Dot Ebi. She consulted Jeanne Benjamin for advice about balancing the many greens. Susan loves Jeanne's spot dyes and bought some that worked perfectly. "Since there is so much green, I decided to hook primitive-style trees, keeping them separated enough to appear as individuals," she said.

She credits Joan Reckwerdt with the advice needed to accurately depict Scooter, the cat hiding in the bushes in the bottom right-hand corner of the rug. And she had to make room for an unexpected guest. "When the rug was almost finished, we adopted a stray dog we named Bingo," says Susan. "I pulled out some grass to make room for her."

Susan wisely kept the border simple. She linked it to other elements through color by bringing in a spot dye similar to that used in the road. The reds in the foreground flowers are the same as the reds colors in the border liner and the Texas flag. Susan used yarn spot dyed with three of the reds from the central design for the outside whipped edge. Adding the Texas Lone Stars was the crowning touch in Susan's tribute to the home place.

Rabbit Hill, *54" x 40", #4- to 6-cut wool on linen. Designed and hooked by Susan Quicksall, Oglesby, Texas, 2001.* IMPACT XPOZURES

The Keddy Place, *54" x 27", hand-dyed and recycled wool and one-ply hand-spun yarn on linen. Designed and hooked by Doris Eaton, Italy Cross, Nova Scotia, 2000.* DORIS EATON

The Keddy Place
Third Place Readers' Choice—Original Design
Doris Eaton

As a rug hooker, Doris Eaton seldom accepts commission work. In fact, she avoids it, worrying that people will not like her interpretation of their ideas. However, when Doris heard Morrey Ewing's request for a rug that featured the lovely old house where he and his wife spent their holidays and summer vacations, Doris knew this was one commission she'd welcome.

Doris listened carefully as Sharon Ewing talked about growing up in Nova Scotia. Doris paid particular attention to the flowers and trees that Sharon loves, as well as what she wanted to plant in her garden. "Her eyes shone so as she talked! I couldn't help but hook the rug that she wanted." The design includes many of Sharon's memories and images, from the hollyhocks, lupines, and crabapple tree at their summer home to the blueberries and delphiniums she had yet to put in the garden there.

Doris had no problem finding sufficient wool on her shelves to complete *The Keddy Place*. Some special dyeing was necessary but most material was used as is. Of special note is the raw sheep's wool spun into a single ply. Doris spot-dyed this with pink and silvery gray-green for the crabapple blossoms, pink and purple for the lupines, and soft greens for the lawn.

A little more than two months after Doris began her work the rug was completed. "I was inspired and couldn't stop working on it," Doris says. "Of all the rugs I've done, this is everyone's favorite."

Silver Compote, *26¹/₂" x 22¹/₂", #3-cut wool on burlap. Designed by Charlotte Stratton; hooked by Peggy Hannum, Lancaster, Pennsylvania, 2001.* IMPACT XPOZURES

Silver Compote
First Place Readers' Choice—Commercial Design
Peggy Hannum

Antiquing for interesting old frames to complement her hooked pieces is one of Peggy's favorite pastimes. She found this frame in a shop in Massachusetts, and for three years, the frame waited patiently in Peggy's workroom.

Then one of her students brought in some old patterns. Peggy's friends and students snatched up most of them, but a few languished on a shelf until Peggy decided to do some cleaning. "I looked through the little pile of burlap patterns and unfolded *Silver Compote*," Peggy says. "Not only was it just what I had envisioned—something with fruit and flowers—but it was the exact size of my gold-leaf frame!"

Nancy Blood helped color plan the project, and Peggy began

dyeing the wool. "The colors blend so well because they are a single family of Triple Over Dyes over different shades of new wool," Peggy says. Her biggest challenge was figuring out how to keep the table and the background from blending together. Her son, an artist, suggested that Peggy hook a slightly lighter shade of the background spot color against the buttonholed darker edge of the table. That touch provided a subtle outline without making the distinction obvious.

Silver Compote was framed by one of Peggy's students, who professionally restored the damaged gold leaf and created a museum-quality framing of the work.

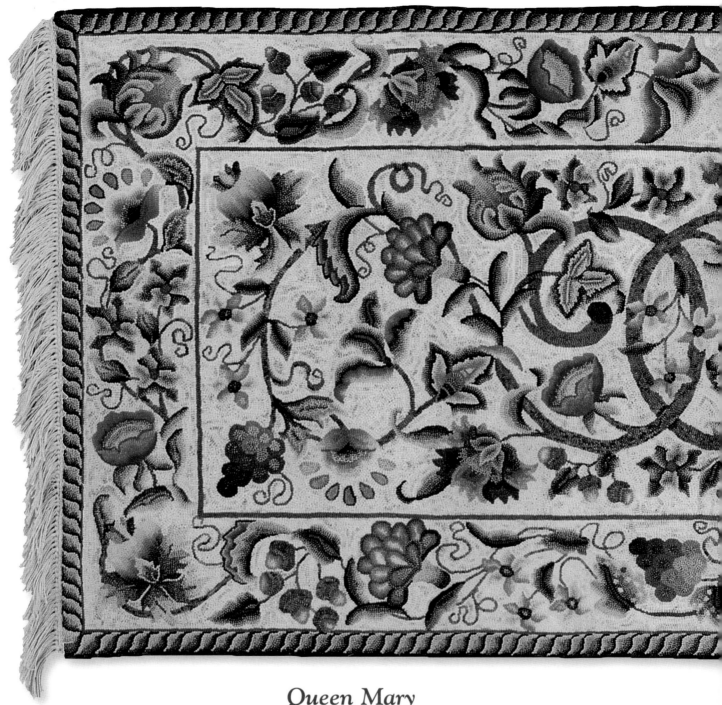

Queen Mary
Second Place Readers' Choice—Commercial Design
Cheryl Meese

Cheryl Meese admired *Queen Mary* for years, ever since she saw a photograph of it on the cover of *The Love and Lure of Hooked Rugs*, by Pearl K. McGown. Every time she finished a project, she considered doing *Queen Mary* next, but was overwhelmed by the size. But she found the trick: "I reminded myself that I really don't like hooking backgrounds, and *Queen Mary* doesn't have much background," she says.

Cheryl is busy with stained glass, cross-stitch, and weaving, but

she has not yet found the time to learn dyeing. She was confident that her teacher, Carol Kassera, would help make this project fun as well as challenging. The two women are friends as well as student and teacher, so color planning was easy. The background is a spot dye, as are most of the branches and twigs; casserole, dip, and gradation dyeing were used for the rest.

The ropelike border was an unpleasant surprise. "The shading is picky, tedious, and repetitive, with many color changes in a

Queen Mary, *67" x 38",
#3- and 4-cut wool on burlap.
Designed by Pearl McGown;
hooked by Cheryl Meese,
Duluth, Minnesota, 2001.*

small area," she explains. "Once you settle into a rhythm, you can get a lot of hooking done in one sitting, but there is an awful lot of rope in this rug." Cheryl made a deal with herself: hooking a motif became the reward for completing a measured amount of rope.

"The cream wool that Carol casserole dyed for the background is absolutely breathtaking," says Cheryl. "It complements the motifs so well and gives the background great depth, warmth, and richness. I hooked it in a #4 cut, but it is still background and, no matter how beautiful, very tedious for me."

"I find that rugs have distinct personalities. They can be sophisticated and elegant, thoughtful and compelling, innocent and funny, warm and agreeable," says Cheryl. "There are as many personalities as there are those hooking them. It is these different characteristics that make this art fascinating and challenging for me."

Collinot
Third Place Readers' Choice—Commercial Design
Sharon Garland

Sharon dedicates *Collinot* to the memory of her mother, a stained glass artist, who died of cancer. "I started hooking this rug while I was caring for her. My color choices were ones she would have loved. She was a great inspiration to me."

Sharon approached her color planning on the fly, saying, "I never color plan the whole rug before I begin. I usually start with a focal point, choose its color, and then evolve my choices for the rest as I go." When Sharon encountered color problems, Virginia Brown helped her make the important decisions. Sharon, who learned to dye as she learned to hook, used dip and jar dyeing for

the all-new #3-cut Dorr wool. Finding the right colors for the flowers was tricky, but Sharon says it was time well spent. She experimented with colors and adapted some of her recipes to get what she wanted by adding just a pinch of dye. "The bluebells and the base are my favorites. The touch of blue adds excitement and really makes it pop, while the olive gives it an antique feel."

She bound the rug's edges with cording, whipped them with wool yarn, and sewed cotton backing to the edge. She used decorative clips with loops and threaded a curtain rod through them so the rug can hang on the wall.

Collinot, *36" x 52", #3-cut wool on cotton. Designed by Jane McGown Flynn. Hooked by Sharon Garland, Hollywood Hills,* *California, 2001.* IMPACT XPOZURES

Celebration XIII—2003

Village of Pemberville
First Place Readers' Choice—Original Design
Cindi Gay

Cindi Gay moved to Pemberville, Ohio, and fell in love with the historic buildings. The night before she was to begin a design class at the Sauder Village Rug Camp, she dashed into town and took photographs of some buildings in the hopes they would serve as a guide for her next rug project.

Cindi started a rug featuring the buildings but had no color plan in the beginning. She eventually needed to decide where she was going and what she needed to dye. "I realized what was bothering me," Cindi says. "All the rich deep reds were on the same side of the rug. Luckily, rug warp has two sides, so I removed the hooking, flipped it over, and tediously redrew the pattern."

Cindi tried various combinations of color, cut, texture, and direction of hooking. She used spot dyes for the buildings' bricks and clapboards. She used spot dyes, textures, and some solids arranged from light to dark.

Cindi feels that all her efforts have been rewarded as she honed her pictorial skills on this rug. "The struggle I went through to master the grass, sky, and pine trees was worth the time," she explains. "The elements that I thought would be difficult turned out to be the simplest."

Village of Pemberville, *36" x 60", multiple cuts of wool on rug warp. Designed and hooked by Cindi Gay, Pemberville, Ohio, 2002.* IMPACT XPOZURES

Best Friends, *16¹/4" x 19¹/2", #3-cut wool on linen. Designed and hooked by Bernice Howell, Beltsville, Maryland, 2002.* IMPACT XPOZURES

Best Friends
Second Place Readers' Choice—Original Design
Bernice Howell

Bernice Howell preserves memories and photographs in wool masterpieces. A photograph taken in 1929 of her brother, Jerry, and their dog on the back steps of their Minnesota farmhouse was an inspiration. And because it was black-and-white, Bernice had the freedom to choose her own colors, relying on her recollections of the setting. She used mostly recycled wool and the swatches she used for facial tones on other projects.

Some parts of the hooking were easy, others were challenging. The dog's fur, made up of a random collection of varied white stripes, tans, and grays, was fun and fairly easy, but her brother's head of tousled curls was more difficult. She wanted to avoid turning it into a solid-looking mass; she ended up giving him four "hair cuts and regrowths" before she was satisfied with the results. "I ended up hooking loosely and letting the porch color show through occasionally," she says. "Another big challenge was his coveralls. There was a lot of trial and error while trying to hook the folds and shadows." She finished the rug by securing museum-quality rag board onto a wood frame and stapling the excess monk's cloth to the back of the frame so that the rug on the front was permanently fastened as a framed picture.

Antique Store in Plymouth, *29" x 37", #3-cut wool on rug warp. Designed and hooked by Fumiyo Hachisuka, Tokyo, Japan, 2002.* IMPACT XPOZURES

Antique Store in Plymouth
Third Place Readers' Choice—Original Design

Fumiyo Hachisuka

One morning after attending a conference in New Bedford, Massachusetts, Fumiyo Hachisuka slipped away to Plymouth to a hotel with a view of the seashore. On an early morning walk into town she discovered the charming antique store now depicted in her rug. The store was not open, but its exterior enchanted this visitor from Japan. "I looked at the store from the outside," she recalls. "It was small but very curious. I took pictures, and I made a pattern from a sketch based on the picture."

Fumiyo added the rocking horse, the sheep, and the teddy bear in the toy cart and placed pieces of china behind the windowpane. These imaginary items made the work more interesting for her to to hook.

She worked to establish the ambience and atmosphere of a real antique store. She decided that her colors would be as close as possible to a reproduction of the real store. She spot and dip dyed new and recycled wool to match the colors on the building and hooked a small piece of white, gray, and black wool cloth to represent the letters on the papers tacked to the door.

The building has many straight lines, so getting a sense of perspective was a challenge, particularly when it came to the building wall. It was important to get the horizonal siding just right. She proceeded carefully and said, "I tried to check my loops by hooking little by little."

Bradley Primitive, *7' x 9', #8-cut wool on linen. Designed by Harry M. Fraser Co.; hooked by Martha W. Adams, Hanover, Virginia, 2001.*

Bradley Primitive
First Place Readers' Choice—Commercial Design
Martha W. Adams

Martha W. Adams loved the scrolls, flowers, and giant leaves of Bradley Primitive so much that when she ordered a larger size of the rug than she meant to, she decided to keep it anyway. "The rug was a challenge in itself, made harder by the fact that I ordered the wrong size," she recalls. "When it arrived in two parts—oh boy."

Martha enjoyed dyeing the wool for *Bradley Primitive* in the new dye kitchen that her husband installed in the basement of their home. She used Pendleton wool skirts for the scrolls in the center and the background and soaked, married, and over dyed brown and green skirts with the color evergreen. The large green leaves were dyed with khaki over light materials, and she used spot dyes in the veins of the leaves.

Martha hooked the piece on a homemade quilting frame set up like a scroll. She worked from the center out, and made certain that each scroll, leaf, and flower was interesting. She finished it with cording and a whipped edge using a combination of green and brown wool yarn.

This particular rug is among Martha's favorites. *Bradley Primitive* won two blue ribbons—best in section and best in show—at the 2001 Virginia State Fair. "The day I ordered it, my husband died from Lou Gehrig's disease," she says. "In his memory, I call it Roy's rug. Hooking it was a labor of love, and it was therapy. This wonderful rug honestly was my life for 11 months."

Charging Elephant, *24" x 24", #3-cut wool on polyester, 2002. Adapted from Steve Bloom's photograph and hooked by Jon Ciemiewicz, Litchfield, New Hampshire, 2002.* STEVE BLOOM

Charging Elephant
Second Place Readers' Choice—Commercial Design

Jon Ciemiewicz

Jon Ciemiewicz didn't have to look far for inspiration. While surfing the Internet, he came upon artist Steve Bloom's Web site and was enthralled with the English photographer's vivid pictures of lions, leopards, and African wildlife. It was the image of the charging elephant that really caught his eye. He has liked elephants since childhood and immediately asked for permission to adapt the photograph.

Using a printed copy of the downloaded picture, Jon drew the image by hand on polyester backing material and then searched through his wool stash for swatches that would fit his color plan. When he wasn't able to find everything he needed, he hand dyed wool using spot, dip, and casserole techniques. "I have hooked in numerous cuts but prefer to design pieces that incorporate

significant detail; #3-cut wool gives me that detail," he explains. "I wanted to create the illusion of cracks and ridges (for the trunk) without having to use small snippets of wool."

The elephant's right ear took a considerable amount of reverse hooking until he got the look he wanted. The dust cloud around the elephant's legs and trunk was especially tough. But the part of his project of which he is most proud is the tusks: he captured the three-dimensional effect he was after.

Charging Elephant took approximately 80 hours over a period of three months to complete, and while most of Jon's past rug creations were given away to family members, this one is proudly displayed in the hallway of his New Hampshire home.

November, *58" x 36", #3-cut wool on rug warp. Designed by Jane McGown Flynn; hooked by Carol Scherer, Dayton, Maryland, 2002.* IMPACT XPOZURES

November
Third Place Readers' Choice—Commercial Design
Carol Scherer

Carol Scherer asked her teacher, Nancy Blood, to come up with a color plan to match a leaf pillow that Carol saw at a rug show. She was thrilled with the Nancy's dyeing results and got to work hooking. She chose rug warp for the backing because she liked its weight and strength.

A challenge for Carol was balancing all that color. As she started the rug, she thought that maybe the yellows, golds, and oranges were too bright. Carol controlled the vibrancy of the bright colors by hooking the lighter values next to the background to "heat it up" and the darker values against the background to "cool it down." She enjoyed balancing the colors and she loves the way all the colors play with each other.

November won a first place award at the Maryland State Fair.

Celebration XIV—2004

Dance of Life
First Place Readers' Choice—Original Design
Cecille Caswell

When looking at Cecille Caswell's exuberantly joyful rug, *Dance of Life*, it's hard to believe that its origins are rooted in tragedy. Cecille began the colorful and lively work of art at a fun-filled rug retreat in the mountains of Alberta, Canada, following the tragic loss of her first hooking teacher—her mother-in-law, Shirley. That loss was coupled with the fact that Cecille was experiencing her own health issues. "I wanted to depict my love of life in a way that also depicts me," says Cecille. "I loved working on this piece. Missing my loved ones was less painful with bright and colorful strips."

Cecille's passion for bright colors and anything funky and nontraditional shows in this rug. She thought the project simple and easy, but discovered that it had its challenges. Initially, she included ribbon and textured yarn as decoration but soon realized that they jumped out too much and were a distraction rather than an embellishment. She ripped them out.

Cecille wanted her lady to glow. To achieve that effect, Cecille put white wool in a shallow pan with a small amount of water and painted from blue to yellow with the back of a spoon. Spot and casserole dyeing enlivened the blues and purples, and Cecille used reds and oranges for the explosion of energy from her exuberant dancing figure. The multi-colored whipped edge was perfect to tie the entire design together.

Dance of Life, *24" x 30", #4- and 5-cut wool on burlap. Designed and hooked by Cecille Caswell, Alberta, Canada, 2003.* BILL BISHOP/IMPACT XPOZURES

Joy Ride, *30" x 27", #3- to 6-cut wool on linen. Designed and hooked by Peggy Northrop, Sebastopal, California, 2003.*
BILL BISHOP/IMPACT XPOZURES

Joy Ride
Second Place Readers' Choice—Original Design
Peggy Northrop

When Peggy Northrop traveled to the Cambria Pines Rug Camp, she packed a suitcase filled with #6-cut wool. She intended to create a landscape fantasy rug representing the hills around her California home. She always liked silly, colorful, and whimsical fiber art, so adding to the rug a frog loosely based on the imported wooden frogs from Bali and Indonesia appealed to her. As Peggy worked on the rug, her teacher advised her to replace the #6 cut with #3 and #4 cuts and do fine shading instead of the blocky colors Peggy had intended.

After camp, Peggy put the project aside. When she picked it up again, she sorted through her wool stash and pulled out all the colors that appealed to her and that seemed to go with any other

color, and any plaid or texture that she liked. "My goal was to have fields in anything but green and to use as many textures and colors as I could," she says. "I had read an article about hooking plaids while retaining their pattern and decided that was also a must for this rug."

Peggy laid out the plaids, textures, dyed, recycled, and new wool on a card table and sorted them into darks, lights, and mediums. She decided to keep a log of all the fabrics and where they were used; she ended up using a total of 207 different pieces of wool for the rug. She wanted to use plaid for the sky but found it to be too busy for around the frog. So she created a cloudy green sky by boiling down and over dyeing some of the plaid.

Russian Birch
Third Place Readers' Choice— Original Design
Gene Shepherd

The landscape that Gene Shepherd recreated in *Russian Birch* was seared into his mind. It was the sort of place, he says, where the "rigid lines of life intersect with a rich fantasy in art, music, and conversation." The piece was a commission for an art collector with a fondness for birch trees.

Gene's client chose the colors to match her home. Gene dyed the wool he used in his magical Russian landscape. The birch wool was spot dyed over an assortment of cream, white, light plaids, and beige colored wool. "My challenge was to do the whole rug in bold perspective with no printed design, using every cut, with just the wool I had dyed," says Gene.

Gene used this commission as an opportunity to experiment with cut size, color, and perspective. Gene wanted to use strong geometric lines in a whimsical pastoral setting. He hooked very wide cuts in the forefront of the piece using vivid colors, and gradually decreased the size with a #3 and a couple of #2s in less intense shading for a feeling of distance. "In one sense, it is a very structured piece," says Gene. "Rigid perspective lines clearly give it movement and direction. However, the perspective lines and outlines of the three main trees were the only pattern lines drawn. I wanted the hooking experience to be something like a walk in the forest—never knowing exactly what would come next—so I left my canvas blank."

Gene hooked in spurts, and ideas often came in a rush. When inspiration ground to a halt, Gene would hang *Russian Birch* in a place where he could study it while doing other things. When ideas began to flow again, he began hooking again. When Gene completed the project, he was surprised and pleased to see that nearly every design element used in the rug's forest floor blended into the room's decor, details that had not been discussed with the client.

Russian Birch, *29¹/₂" x 66", #2- to 10-cut wool on monk's cloth. Designed and hooked by Gene Shepherd, Anaheim, California, 2003.* BILL BISHOP/IMPACT XPOZURES

Eighteenth-Century Fable
First Place Readers' Choice—
Commercial Design
Patricia Seliga

One look at *Eighteenth-Century Fable* and it's easy to see that this rug hooker didn't mind a challenge. After hooking a dozen small projects, Patricia Seliga was ready to tackle a big one. She loved the large size of the piece and she looked forward to all the interesting details in the design, including the fairies. She thought they might be tricky but, to her delight, "they just seemed to hook themselves. They were such fun." The rug was full of interest and movement and Patricia had lots of opportunities to experiment with color and techniques.

With so many colors in the rug—the greens for the hillsides, the blues for the sky, the yellow branches for the border—it was challenging to find a common color scheme. She unified the rug by using red for the clothing, while still giving each woman her own style despite using such similar shades.

Patricia hooked mostly in #5- and #6- cut wool because she wanted a folk art look rather than fine shading details. One of the many lessons she learned from hooking *18th Century Fable* was how to estimate how much wool a large rug needs and how to improvise when you run short of wool. "I also learned that each little detail adds to the design," explains Patricia. "Adding something different to each critter and animal gave them personalities."

Patricia chose this pattern because of all the detail and the opportunities and possibilites for color and technique. The sheer size was a challenge; coupled with the incredible detail in the pattern it was a challenge this hooker could not resist.

Eighteenth-Century Fable, *88" x 64", #5- and 6-cut wool on monk's cloth. A Harry M. Fraser pattern; hooked by Patricia Seliga, St. Louis, Missouri, 2003.* BILL BISHOP/IMPACT XPOZURES

Istanbul, *60" round, #3- and 4-cut wool on linen. Designed by Pearl K. McGown; hooked by Peggy Hannum, Lancaster, Pennsylvania, 2003.* BILL BISHOP/IMPACT XPOZURES

Istanbul
Second Place Readers' Choice—Commercial Design
Peggy Hannum

Several years ago, Peggy's rug hooking teacher suggested that she hook this colorful design. Just hearing the name Istanbul conjured up the mysteries of the exotic Middle East, a part of the world she and her husband knew well. "We lived in Jerusalem for three years as liaisons for the United Methodist Church," Peggy says. "We visited Istanbul several times in our travels."

One summer, Peggy's roommate at the McGown Northern Teachers' Workshop had some patterns she was disposing of and one of them was *Istanbul.* Peggy decided right then that she would make this rug her next project.

The rug was a delight to hook because there were no parts of the design that were repeated. She sent the pattern to her teacher,

Nancy Blood, for color planning; she decided on 16 different 8-value swatches. Peggy loves dyeing almost as much as hooking, so she had a lot of fun dyeing the wool and spot dyeing the background.

She found it difficult to hook the two birds and their mass of feathers; because there was not much definition in the 8-value swatches, the feathers seemed to melt into each other. She used a technique she learned years ago where thread from a darker piece of wool can be hooked around each feather. "It's a process that sounds deadly, but in fact is easy and fast," says Peggy. "One hooks in existing holes and not in every one, giving the illusion of an edge without it becoming a definite outline."

Square Harmony, *52" x 32", #8-cut wool on linen. Designed by Monika Jones; hooked by Connie Baar, Tempe, Arizona, 2003.*
BILL BISHOP/IMPACT XPOZURES

Square Harmony
Third Place Readers' Choice—Commercial Design
Connie Baar

Connie Baar loves red and other rich, vibrant colors. Brilliant hues and all the colors of the rainbow are common in her home, which is decorated in red with mustard and olive accents. *Square Harmony* has everything that Connie likes in a rug—those exhilarating colors incorporated in a pattern with both geometric and floral elements. "I chose this pattern for its variety of motifs," Connie says. "This rug was a lot of fun, and it held my interest to the finish."

Connie began hooking *Square Harmony* in a workshop taught by Monika Jones. She mostly #8-cut and #6-cut over-dyed new wool. Connie had Monika's original rug to look at while she hooked, though the rugs are quite different in color and hooking style. Studying the Monika's rug helped Connie plan her own masterpiece.

Connie is particularly proud of the rug's energy and the background, where the appearance of uneven fading comes from as-is textures. She threw out the rule book and relied on her imagination to hook some of the flowers and leaves for her own primitive shading. Connie finished *Square Harmony* by folding the linen forward and then whipstitching it with thick wool yarn.

Celebration XV—2005

Night Watch, *40" x 40", #5- and 6-cut wool on linen. Designed and hooked by Dianne Landberg, Bend, Oregon, 2003.* BILL BISHOP/IMPACT XPOZURES

Night Watch
First Place Readers' Choice—Original Design
Dianne Landberg

Dianne Landberg's inspiration for *Night Watch* came from her own deep faith. "It grew out of a repeating scene in my head of a flock of sheep in the deep darkness, touched by the light of an unseen moon, watched over by trusted guardians," explains Dianne. "It was a vision I couldn't get out of my head. It wanted to be done."

Dianne began gathering the recycled wool that she needed to make her dream come alive. For Dianne, hooking is simply painting with wool, and she wanted to emphasize the sculptural quality of the rug by spot dyeing and dip dying some of the wool. She wanted a rugged feel but also wanted it to appear surreal, so she used #5 and #6 cuts and tried not to overdo the details. One hooking challenge was to make the baby sheep look sleepy and innocent. Through trial and error, she found that subtle shading was the answer.

The mother-baby interaction is her favorite part of the rug. She loved the sense that the two feel complete safety and comfort while the rams watch over them.

It's a Keeper, *50" x 30", #4- to 6-cut wool on linen. Designed and hooked by Patricia Van Arsdale, Floyds Knobs, Indiana, 2004.*
BILL BISHOP/IMPACT XPOZURES

It's a Keeper
Second Place Readers' Choice—Original Design
Patricia Van Arsdale

Patricia Van Arsdale hooked *It's a Keeper* to honor her husband's achievement in becoming a certified and licensed professional fishing guide on Lake Cumberland in Kentucky. "One day I saw a page which pictured a large array of fish in an encyclopedia-like fashion," recalls Patricia. "All the fish were heading in one direction. The Latin names and a description of the species were included, and I thought it was beautiful. I was sure my husband would love a fish rug."

Patricia used recycled wools for the fish and dyed the green spot and dip dyed the blue for the border. She loved the eye of the largest fish because it looked so real. "The critters in the corners added some fun and turned out better than I expected," says Patricia. "But I think it's the sculpted rope that gets the most attention, and I enjoy sharing how it was done.

But this fun-loving rug turned out to be anything but fun. The problem was estimating wool quantity and knowing how much of each color she needed. Patricia ran out of the first background wool, which was the plaid. She couldn't replace it, so she chose a herringbone pattern instead in a near color of blue. She then had to pluck out a lot of the plaid and re-hook it in random spots while hooking in the new herringbone. Then she ran out of the green spot-dyed wool. She re-dyed the wool but couldn't quite make it match. Again she found herself plucking and re-hooking. Then she ran out of the blue herringbone in the background. Fortunately, she was able to reorder it and she was back in business. "Now I overestimate the quantity of wool I think I will need and then add even more," remarks Patricia.

Hydrangeas & Lace, *32" x 21", #3- and 4-cut wool on rug warp. Designed and hooked by Gina Conway, Ridgefield, Washington, 2004.*

Hydrangeas and Lace
Third Place Readers' Choice—Original Design
Gina Conway

Gina Conway, a professional artist and floral designer, loves to hook fine-cut, shaded floral and traditional rugs with scrolls. Her inspiration for *Hydrangeas and Lace* came from a design she painted on a sink in her newly remodeled bathroom, and the design from the sink came from the hydrangeas blooming right outside her window. "The hydrangea flowers were very different to hook than they were to paint," Gina remarks. "From hooking this rug, I learned to simplify my patterns and not draw so many details."

Gina did all the color planning, and casserole dyed the leaves and spot dyed the stems and background. For the hydrangeas, Gina added swatches using Triple Over Dye (TOD) novelty dye formulas, but her biggest challenge was to make light flowers and dark flowers as the hydrangeas overlapped.

Gina used new wool instead of recycled wool. She lives only 30 miles from a Pendleton Woolen Mill outlet, and the women who work there know that Gina turns the wool she buys into amazing works of art. "I take finished pieces in to show them what it is I do with their wool," says Gina. "They are constantly amazed and are becoming educated in what weights of wool will work in the rugs."

Hydrangeas and Lace was the third rug Gina created with a lace edge, a technique she had been practicing for a while. To finish off the rug—a step that she doesn't particularly enjoy—Gina had someone else use a wool binding technique that she learned from a friend's mother who was a quilter and rug hooker.

Gina's experience and talents as a professional porcelain artist and floral designer is put to good use in her hooking. It is no wonder that she prefers to hook fine-cut shaded florals and scrolls, though she has also hooked #7 cut primitives. She says that "I try to educate all I come in contact with about rug hooking. I have a few friends who call me an 'apostle' of rug hooking and say I'm proselytizing." *Hydrangeas & Lace* is a truly wonderful way to spread the word about the creativity and wonder of rug hooking.

A Walk in the Jungle, *34" x 48", #3-cut wool on monk's cloth. Designed by Hues Views; hooked by Judy Colley, Wyoming, Michigan, 2004.* BILL BISHOP/IMPACT XPOZURES

A Walk in the Jungle
First Place Readers' Choice—Commercial Design
Judy Colley

Judy Colley's rug, *A Walk in the Jungle*, is way out of her comfort zone. In her 33 years of rug hooking, Judy has always hooked florals and Orientals using fine cuts of wool. With its lush foliage and stalking big cats, *A Walk in the Jungle* was very different. "I've hooked flowers and leaves before, but I have never hooked animals," Judy explains. "I chose this design because it was a well-drawn, well-balanced pattern. That's always a big plus."

Hooking the lush foliage came easy as Judy has hooked gardens of leaves and flowers many times. But the feline faces presented a challenge. "I wanted them to look as real as possible and used lots of visual aids and pictures for all types of cats to help me. " Judy also appreciated the help she got from her teacher, Diane Stoffel, especially for choosing the vivid colors in her jungle. Judy elicited some help with the color planning, did her own spot dyeing, and

incorporated a lot of leftover pieces from other projects. She used some as-is checks and plaids.

Realism was important to Judy, and it was also her biggest challenge. She studied pictures of cats, pictures of eyes, and used other visual aids to help her as she planned. She wanted to show the powerful shoulders and outstanding musculature of the animals; she wanted the animals to look like they were really walking through the jungle. Judy used different shades in the big cats' bodies—seven colors in the eyes alone. All of that preparation and focus on color and shading taught Judy that rug hookers can hook anything an artist can paint.

Judy finished the rug by whipping its edges with dyed-to-match wool yarn. The whole project took four months, and she finds that she wouldn't mind hooking another animal rug in the future.

Culley's Cottage, *30¹/₂" x 24¹/₂", #3- to 6-cut wool on linen. Designed by George Culley; hooked by Trish Johnson, Fergus, Ontario, Canada, 2004.* BILL BISHOP/IMPACT XPOZURES

Culley's Cottage
Second Place Readers' Choice—Commercial Design
Trish Johnson

For Trish, rugs are art. They are also visual diaries, meaningful to the fiber artist, telling his or her own personal story. Although *Culley's Cottage* is someone else's design, rug hooker Trish Johnson added her own elements as part of a teaching project on how to personalize a commercial pattern. "We all had the same pattern," Trish explains, "but we each depicted a different season and added personal elements of our own."

She changed the house to an arts-and-crafts–style cottage, an architectural style that Trish admires. She added the stone fireplace, the two stained glass windows on each side, and emphasized the veranda. "The windows are reminiscent of (our) first home together," remarks Trish. "Verandas make a house seem friendlier." Trish add water to the design, reminiscent of her

childhood home by the river. Trish changed the focal point of the rug to the human figure, her son shoveling snow, rather than the cottage.

Trish did all the color planning, choosing complementary tones shown in nature rather than true blacks or true whites. She is a realist and likes things that aren't too perfect or matched up. "I try to restrict my palette and am not much for subtlety. I believe you shouldn't try to use every color."

Trish used a variety of fabrics for *Culley's Cottage,* including some new wool. The snow was an Anne Klein jacket—a white bouclé blend of wool and alpaca. The fireplace stones are tweeds from a plaid scarf, the chimney smoke is lopi wool, and the burgundy of the cottage is from an over-dyed red skirt.

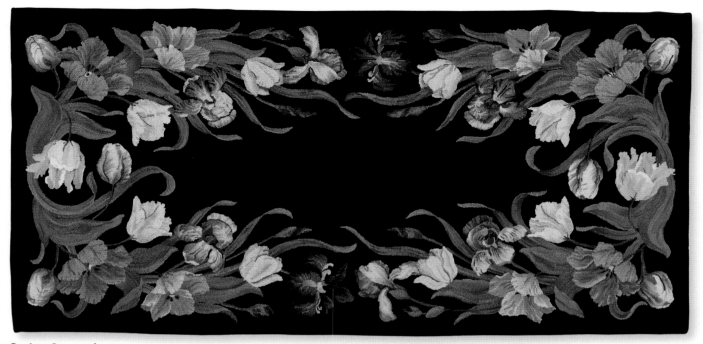

Spring Serenade, *90" x 45", #6-cut wool on rug warp. Designed by Heirloom Rugs; hooked by Marilyn Gibbs, Hartville, Ohio, 2004.* BILL BISHOP/IMPACT XPOZURES

Spring Serenade
Third Place Readers' Choice—Commercial Design
Marilyn Gibbs

Marilyn Gibbs knows how to make a good trade. When she was ready to put an addition on her house, Marilyn traveled to her brother's Vermont home carrying pattern catalogs from her Buckeye Rug Hooking Guild. The deal was that her brother and sister-in-law could choose any rug they wanted and she would hook it in exchange for her brother's architectural plan and design for an addition to Marilyn's home.

When her sister-in-law saw *Spring Serenade* in the Heirloom catalog, she had no need to search any further. "She especially liked the motion it displays," Marilyn recalls. "She requested the dark green background, purple irises, and some yellow tulips. Everything else was up to me."

Marilyn got to work color planning the rug. Her camera was always close by and she took many photographs of irises, iris buds, and tulips in her garden and growing along the road. Marilyn used the 8-jar method for some of the tulips and dip dyed the greens for the iris and tulip leaves and iris flowers. For the purple, yellow, and pink closed tulips, Marilyn dip dyed the wool strips purple on one end, yellow on the opposite, and pink in the middle by holding the ends and dipping into the pink dye bath. "The two yellow open parrot tulips were most challenging to shade. I sought the help of fellow guild members, added white, and reverse hooked parts of them several times."

Towers & Turrets, Queen's University
First Place Readers' Choice—Original Design

Catherine Henning

Catherine Henning's connections to Queen's University in Kingston, Ontario, run deep. She attended school there. Nearby is St. Andrew's Presbyterian Church where Catherine's family were members, where she and her husband married, and where both daughters were christened.

Catherine took pictures of the school in the winter. With no leaves on the trees, she captured the clear lines of the buildings. There was some snow at the time, so Catherine designed the four seasons into the project. She used artistic license and hooked the campus from her memories of it during the 1950s. She used the actual walkways around St. Andrew's to join each of the buildings' paths with the church. She added flowerbeds and trees to Grant Hall with its bell tower, where exams and graduation ceremonies were held. Douglas Library, shown diagonally across from Grant Hall, incorporated fall colors. Ontario Hall and Old Meds Building are shown in a summer setting.

Catherine worked on this rug on and off from 1998 to 2005.

Towers and Turrets, Queen's University, *47" x 67", #4-cut wool on monk's cloth. Designed and hooked by Catherine Henning, Burlington, Ontario, 2005.* BILL BISHOP/IMPACT XPOZURES

My Mémère—
A Strong Woman

Second Place Readers' Choice—
Original Design

Carol Koerner

Art has always been as much a part of Carol Koerner's life as breathing. She drew, painted, built, or sewed as a child and considered herself a watercolorist as an adult until she discovered rug hooking. Now, she can see how all the principles of art come into play in each piece she hooks.

Her rug, *My Mémère—A Strong Woman*, called upon all her artistic skills. "This is my great-grandmother, Georgianna Emond, truly a strong woman," says Carol. "Mémère was our French-Canadian name for Grandmother. She could do everything except read and write. She died at nearly 100 years old when I was 25. I didn't realize how much she influenced me until I began this piece."

Carol transferred her favorite picture to a linen background using Red Dot Tracer, and then dyed her fabrics. She used 11 shades of flesh colors in the face and arms, and she tried to show Mémère's rimless glasses without actually outlining them. She used several shades of creamy white, blue, and green for the dress.

The rug's background was challenging. She wanted Mémère's white clapboard house in the background, but she had to gray it down so it could recede visually and not interfere with the whites of the hair and dress.

It took Carol about five months to complete the rug, and while many of Carol's family members also have sweet memories of Mémère and would like to have the rug, Carol decided that this is a rug she will treasure.

My Mémère—A Strong Woman, *17" x 28", #3-cut wool on linen. Designed and hooked by Carol Koerner, Bethesda, Maryland, 2005.* BILL BISHOP/IMPACT XPOZURES

Leaf Puzzle
Third Place Readers' Choice— Original Design
Joyce Krueger

For many years, Joyce Krueger wanted to hook a rug that looked like a pile of fall leaves. She thinks that nothing compares to the childhood joy at the crunch and crackle of a heap of autumn foliage cushioning a flying leap. "I saved wools for this project for about five years," says Joyce. "Every time I saw a piece of wool that looked like an autumn leaf, I put it aside. It was one of those rugs that kept calling me."

Joyce collaborated with Jeanne Field and dyed the new and recycled wool using dip, casserole, and onion skin dyeing. She loved every single leaf she hooked, but if pressed to pick a favorite, it would have to be the large yellow leaves. "These were hooked with recycled wool that I over dyed with onion skins," says Joyce. "I hooked the wool in the order it was cut. The result was patches of color that look like the leaves when they fall off the tree."

The design has so many overlapping images that it is no wonder that she had to resolve some problems during the four months it took to complete *Leaf Puzzle*. The biggest challenge was to keep track of what leaf was on top of the next leaf. In order to make the design, Joyce enlarged the leaf motifs, cut them out, and taped them in place on a large piece of paper. She covered the whole pattern with a sticky clear plastic so the leaves wouldn't move. After she transferred the design to the monk's cloth, all she could see was a bunch of shapes with veins in them. "In order to tell which leaf I was working on, I had to refer back to the paper pattern," Joyce explains. "I color planned as I went along. It reinforced the fact that you cannot completely color plan a rug like this before you start hooking."

Leaf Puzzle, *39" x 27$\frac{1}{2}$", #5- and 6-cut wool on monk's cloth. Designed and hooked by Joyce Krueger, Waukesha, Wisconsin, 2004.*

BILL BISHOP/IMPACT XPOZURES

Alphapets
First Place Readers' Choice—Commercial Design
Lucille Sanders

When Lucille Sanders first came upon *Alphapets* in a 1995 issue of *Rug Hooking* magazine, she knew it was the perfect blend of her interests. On the one hand, it's a presentation of animals in alphabetical order, beginning with aardvark and ending with zebra. On the other hand, it presented interesting challenges and allowed her to use up some of the surplus wool that she had accumulated through the years.

Alphapets was more of a challenge than she anticipated. The commercial pattern included only a simple outline on the backing, so Lucille did a shaded pencil sketch of each animal based on photos from magazines and the Internet. Once she had an animal's contour, she chose the colors she needed. Then she chose the backgrounds so that each animal had its own habitat which would transition smoothly into the next. "The warm oranges and yellows

of the kangaroo outback had to give way to greens of the steamy jungle, browns of the African grasslands, and the night sky of the owl," Lucille says. "The rug made me use everything I knew about blending colors, and my knowledge of why some combinations were pleasing and some were not."

Probably most challenging for Lucille were the skies that extended the full width from the African desert to the howling jackal on the mountaintop. She succeeded in connecting those sky elements, which tied the whole picture together.

Lucille didn't use as much of that surplus wool as she had hoped. "I now have left over leftovers," she remarks. "However, I did learn a lot about over dyeing. Since the amount of wool needed for each animal was so small, I could dabble to my heart's content."

Alphapets, *32" x 57", #3- and 4-cut wool on burlap. Designed by Muzzy Petrow; hooked by Lucille Sanders, Lancaster, Pennsylvania, 2005.* BILL BISHOP/IMPACT XPOZURES

Blythe Shoals, *38" x 31", #3- and 4-cut wool on rug warp. Designed by Margaret Hunt Masters; hooked by Carla Fortney, Glendale, California, 2004.* BILL BISHOP/IMPACT XPOZURES

Blythe Shoals
Second Place Readers' Choice—Commercial Design
Carla Fortney

*B*lythe Shoals is Carla Fortney's third rug and her first attempt at shaded flowers. When her aunt and her mom heard about Carla's love for the Dutch Old Masters' floral paintings, they told her to take a class with Sibyl Osicka, who told Carla that she had just the right pattern.

Sibyl planned the colors for the rug, and she dyed many exquisitely shaded swatches, including a 12-value swatch for the fabric on the table on which the beautiful vase of blooms rests. A lighter spot dye was used for the overall background and a darker one for behind the flowers.

Carla made some changes to the pattern. She added more grapes, made the tulip larger, and added the suggestion of a few more stems. And she changed the straight line separating the table from the background, which she thought was too stiff and unnatural, to an undulating line, giving the folds more depth and realism.

Carla loved working on this rug because of its challenges and how it was constantly changing. "By the time I got to the pink fabric, I felt pretty comfortable with shading, and the 12-vaule swatch allowed me to get great contrast," says Carla. "I worked this part from left to right and I'm really proud of the folds on the right."

Willowbank, *70" x 50", #3-cut wool on rug warp. Designed by Jane McGown Flynn; hooked by Jean Cooper, Southhold, New York, 2004.*

Willowbank
Third Place Readers' Choice—Commercial Design
Jean Cooper

Crewel and oriental rugs are Jean's Cooper's favorites, and sometimes she'll hook a geometric pattern. With *Willowbank*, Jean was able to combine the best of all of those styles into one large rug.

She used many dyeing techniques and color formulas—including spot, Jacobean, and Imari formulas—to ensure that the rug coordinated with the draperies in her studio. The most challenging part was finding a red and purple recipe that could co-star with all of the other colors playing supporting roles. "To marry a red and a purple, I found formulas that had a common dye," Jean recalls. "Then I knew they wouldn't clash. But it took a multitude of dye bath tryouts."

Although *Willowbank* is a commercial pattern, Jean added a few creative touches of her own. She hooked the border from another rug called *Neville Sisters* and added it to *Willowbank*. Jean liked the two outer borders, and although she says they were intricate to hook, she feels that they draw the whole rug together.

The Apple Girl, *20" x 31", #3- and 4-cut wool on rug warp. Adapted from a greeting card and hooked by Barbara Lekstrom, Annandale, Virginia, 2004.* BILL BISHOP/IMPACT XPOZURES

The Apple Girl
First Place Readers' Choice—Adaptation
Barbara Lekstrom

Barbara Lekstrom loves creating faces in rugs and truly enjoys capturing personalities through facial expressions. And her experience making Scandinavian character dolls with molded clay faces helps her with her rug hooking as she strives to hook realistic faces. In *The Apple Girl*, Barbara captured the exuberance of the child who, with an endearing look and outstretched hand, is offering the viewer a piece of fruit. Barbara has perfected the shading and shadowing of skin colors. Her subject appears to come alive and is ready to step off the rug.

Barbara designed *The Apple Girl* from a Christmas card. Color planning was easy because she stayed with the colors on the card. She used swatches and a light spot dye over new wool for the background. The red dress was the biggest challenge. Barbara wanted to show movement when the little girl moved her arm forward and out. Her subtle shading techniques in the dress folds suggest the softness of the cloth and movement as the little girl reaches toward the viewer.

Deere & Co., 200 Years of Progress, *23³/4" x 37", #2- and 3-cut wool and threadwork on rug warp. Adapted from an 1877 poster for Deere & Co. and hooked by Elizabeth Marino, South Egremont, Massachusetts, 2005.*

Deere & Co., 200 Years of Progress
Second Place Readers' Choice—Adaptation
Elizabeth Marino

Sometimes even an accomplished rug hooker is daunted by the project she's chosen. This was the case with Elizabeth Marino and her unusual wall hanging depicting an old advertisement for the John Deere Company. Elizabeth took nearly three years to complete *Deere & Co., 200 Years of Progress.*

Elizabeth is a descendant of the company's founder, John Deere. Her father worked for the company, and Elizabeth grew up in Moline, Illinois, the home of the company's corporate headquarters. Given that family connection and her love for hooking

pictorials, she and her husband looked at old advertisements from the history of the company. She chose a few images and then contacted the reference archivist at Deere & Company to ask for permission to transform one of them into a rug. Elizabeth got the go-ahead for her project and received a black-and-white photograph of the advertisement she would use for her pattern. This original artwork was in honor of the 75th anniversary of the company's birth. Fortunately Elizabeth located a color version of the advertisement and she stayed as faithful to the original as possible.

Temptation, *28″ x 44″, #3-cut wool on monk's cloth. Adapted from a John H. Dells painting and hooked by Valerie Johnston, Wilmington, North Carolina, 2005.*
BILL BISHOP/IMPACT XPOZURES

Temptation
Third Place Readers' Choice—Adaptation
Valerie Johnston

Valerie Johnston found this picture irresistible. "It made me feel so happy whenever I looked at it that I knew it had to be a rug," says Valerie. "I waited three years before I started it because I didn't feel confident in my ability. I learned a lot in that time and am very glad I waited."

Valerie and Judy Quintman planned the colors and stayed as close to the original picture as they could. In addition to new wool, Valerie used heavy thread for the bunny's and guinea pig's whiskers. Creating the baskets was a challenge. "I love baskets, and since they were a big part of the picture, I really wanted to get them just right," recalls Valerie. "I met the challenge with attention to detail and shading with the wool."

Overall, Valerie found the rug a real joy to work on from the beginning to the end. It kept her interest and she thought about what she would be working on snext even when she wasn't hooking. Anticipation is half the fun of starting a new rug, especially when the end result is just what she had hoped for.

Celebration XVII—2007

Helio's Harvest, *24″ x 36″, #5-cut wool on linen burlap. Designed and hooked by Laura Boszormeny, Brockville, Ontario, Canada,* 2005. BILL BISHOP/IMPACT XPOZURES

Helio's Harvest
First Place Readers' Choice—Original Design
Laura Boszormeny

Laura Boszormeny is not hesitant to proclaim that *Helio's Harvest* is the best thing she has ever designed and hooked. Sunflowers are a personal favorite, and she says that the excitement in these sunflowers is the culmination of 30 years of learning, dyeing, hooking, and teaching. "I have hooked several pieces with sunflowers," Laura says.

Laura liked to hook large flowers, so she drew the sunflowers and leaves in *Helio's Harvest* big, bold, and effervescent. She chose a strong gold color that makes a strong statement; the dazzling flowers come alive. The three-dimensional effect of the petals comes from dip dyeing 36"- to 40"-long pieces of wool.

She also dip dyed 18" pieces of wool for the leaves. Laura calls the design "painterly." The bouncy, colorful sunflowers appear to sway and grow right in front of you.

Laura likes to include something from her instructors in her rugs, and *Helio's Harvest* is no exception. Between the leaves is an antique black spot dye done by her teacher, Jeanne Field, during the Magnificent Multi Flora course at the Trent School of Rug Hooking where Laura created this rug. This rug was so much fun for Laura and such a satisfying project that she hopes to teach a course in impressionistic flowers to her St. Lawrence College class.

Magnolia Mix
Second Place Readers' Choice—Original Design
Capri B. Jones

Magnolia Mix is a painterly rug, and Capri Boyle Jones is the artist. Capri used her hook as a paintbrush and the luscious wools are the paints. The flowers in this rug shimmer and move toward the light as they take on life against the backdrop of lush green leaves. Even the hummingbird hovering over the flower seems to be real.

The idea for this piece came when Capri asked her husband what type of rug he would like. "Something with magnolias," he replied. That's all she had to hear. With 16 years of rug hooking experience behind her, she began the project, choosing several magnolia varieties. "The magnolias represented in the design, beginning with the southern magnolia in the lower right and moving clockwise, include the cucumber tree fruit, Japanese magnolia, sweet bay magnolia, and the lily tree," explains Capri. "The

Magnolia Mix, *48" x 26", #3-cut wool on English linen.*
Designed and hooked by Capri B. Jones, Navarre, Florida, 2005.
BILL BISHOP/IMPACT XPOZURES

clumps of leaves are representative of the southern magnolia."

Capri dyed all new wool for the project, using 6-value swatches for the flowers, fruit, and leaves. To finish the rug, she used a combination of acid-free adhesive, stitching, and wool thread (for whipping) and binding tape.

Capri's favorite part of the rug is the unusual border. She learned a lot creating the cutout shapes but it required meticulous handwork and thought. Capri also likes the depth within the clumps of leaves. To balance the colors she planned the color locations for the entire rug before hooking and she labeled the colors on the rug. It now graces the bedroom wall in Capri's home to the delight of her husband who originally placed the order.

Three Skyes, *29^1/$_2$″ x 29^1/$_2$″, #3- and 5-cut wool on linen. Designed and hooked by Marian Hall, West Chester, Pennsylvania, 2006.*

Three Skyes
Third Place Readers' Choice—Original Design
Marian Hall

The three very cute dogs that were the inspiration for this rug belong to Marian's friend in Cornwall, England. Marian wanted to see if she could capture the irresistible expressions and cuteness of this trio of Skye Terriers and their personalities in wool. Any Skye terrier owner will tell you that these faithful companions are fearless, good-tempered, loyal, friendly with those he knows, and somewhat cautious with those he doesn't. Marian posed each one to peek out through well-feathered hair in its own unique way.

Marian's favorite is the black dog. She loves the face of the middle canine, which turned out to be the most demanding part of this rug. "The challenge was how to show features on a black dog with black eyes and black nose, totally covered in long, shaggy,

black hair." Marian used a different color to define those features that would have otherwise disappeared.

Marian captured the style, elegance, and sturdiness of this terrier breed from Scotland. She challenged herself to capture the different colorings of each. She planned the colors and dyed all the wool using a combination of spot, dip, and casserole methods and found the perfect green for the background. "Always start with more background wool than you think you will need," Marian advised. "I ran out of dark green and had to dye more and match it to finish the border."

Marian hooks primitive-style rugs in a finer cut, and enjoys the challenge of fine shading. *Three Skyes* was a true test of these interests; these shaggy dogs are a testament to her skill.

Hi There, *31" x 26", #3-cut wool on monk's cloth. Designed by Jane Olson; hooked by Roland C. Nunn, Orinda, California, 2005.*
BILL BISHOP/IMPACT XPOZURES

Hi There
First Place Readers' Choice—Commercial Design
Roland Nunn

Six years ago, Roland's granddaughters, Emily and Kimberly, asked their grandfather to teach them how to hook rugs. Roland let them choose a design and they picked a McGown gingham dog and calico cat. Over the next two years, with some help and lots of encouragement from Roland, both girls completed their patterns, which are proudly on display in their home.

Each then asked Roland to hook a pattern especially for them. Using a selection of greeting cards, Emily picked a pattern with a dog and butterfly, and Kimberly selected this raccoon and ground squirrel design. Despite the whimsy and clearly defined objects in the design, Roland discovered that the most difficult part of the pattern was selecting swatch colors and brightness, particularly for the raccoons and the fallen log. He considered those images the central theme in the story of the rug. Roland took his time with the project and took five months to complete the hooking.

Roland has completed over 50 rugs in all types of styles: geometrics, Orientals, florals, animals, landscapes, and scrolls. What began as a sit-down hobby—reminding him of his own mother hooking in the 1950s—has brought him into his own rewarding fiber arts world. He hopes his granddaughters will one day hook as well.

Tiger, *21" x 21", #3- and 4-cut wool on monk's cloth. Designed by Jon Ciemiewicz; hooked by Judy Carter, Willow Street,* *Pennsylvania, 2006.* BILL BISHOP/IMPACT XPOZURES

Tiger
Second Place Readers' Choice—Commercial Design
Judy Carter

The eyes are the key to a rug like this, and those eyes are Judy's favorite part of *Tiger*. "I started with the eyes, which were actually the easiest part of the rug," she says. "I used three values of one color for the pupil and the highlight. The eyes draw you into the rug."

Judy took a class with Jon Ciemiewicz and wanted a tiger to go with the lion she was working on, so she asked Jon for a design. Teacher and student planned the colors; while Jon dyed wool, Judy added textures to achieve the look she wanted. She learned that textured wool gave her more realistic results when hooking fur, and clearly Judy was successful in that endeavor. Half of the more than 20 different wools in the tiger are textures.

Judy's biggest challenges were hooking the whiskers and the mane. She wanted the whiskers to stand out. The problem was that the color she chose for the whiskers was the same color as parts of the tiger's mane. She hooked the whiskers first, then the mane under them. After the mane was hooked, she pulled out the whiskers and re-hooked them so they would be more prominent.

Trout Stream, *44" x 34", #3- and 5-cut wool on rug warp. Designed by Elizabeth Black; hooked by Georgia A. Prosser, Shelby, North Carolina, 2006.* BILL BISHOP/IMPACT XPOZURES

Trout Stream
Third Place Readers' Choice—Commercial Design
Georgia A. Prosser

Georgia A. Prosser wanted to create a rainbow trout rug for her son. So she took the rainbow trout idea to Elizabeth Black who created the design. Elizabeth surrounded the fish with seaweed and rocks so it appeared to be hanging in midair. The design thrilled Georgia, but as she eyed the wool for the gorgeous underwater scene, she wondered if she was capable of doing it justice.

The water was fun to hook, but the biggest challenge was the rainbow trout. Blending the colors properly and lining up the dots on the tail took time. Georgia worked hard to make sure that the dots stayed symmetrical as they arced over the fish.

Georgia wanted the finishing touches to blend in perfectly. Instead of using binding tape, Georgia used an over-dyed piece of wool which was cut on the bias so that the seams for the whole length going around the rug would blend in. She attached the wool to the rug before she finished hooking it so that she could hook right up to the edge.

The Gleaners, *12" x 16", #3- to 6-cut wool on linen. Adapted from Jean Francois Millet's painting and hooked by Linda Fernandes, South Lyon, Michigan, 2006.* LINDA FERNANDES

The Gleaners
First Place Readers' Choice—Adaptation
Linda Fernandes

Linda Fernandes's *The Gleaners* is based on the 1857 artwork of French painter Jean Francois Millet, who depicted rural life in 19th century France in *Les Glaneuses (The Gleaners)*. The painting shows three hunched-over female figures gathering the harvest's leftovers, poor women gleaning the last of the crop in the field. "The rug was done as a dedication to the mission of feeding the poor," Linda says.

Linda enjoys dyeing her own wool, but she also loves using as-is textures for the warmth that they give to a rug. She was to use all her skills when she tackled this project.

Linda used the work of art as her color plan. She had some obstacles to overcome if she wanted to transform the French masterpiece into wool, specifically the size of the strip she chose to hook with. Linda always hooked primitive wide cut designs, but her rug adaptation required smaller pieces. Linda consulted with her teacher and friend, Dianne Klamik, who suggested that Linda complete a section of the design and then return for a critique. That process worked, and as she continued with each section, the rug came to life. Using smaller cuts than she was used to, Linda was delighted at how real the women in the field looked, and she loved the shading that she achieved.

"The experience of hooking a fine cut piece gives me a different eye when choosing color and texture for my primitives—still aged but different," she says.

She serged the edges and stretched the wool-on-linen depiction over stretching bars. Then Linda had the rug framed at a gallery. *The Gleaners* is on display at the Gleaners Community Food Bank of southeastern Michigan. It is a reminder of the work to be done for the people who need care, and it pays homage to those who take on the task of helping others.

Bill—Circa 1931, 15" x 19", #3- and 4-cut wool on rug warp. Adapted from a family photograph of her husband and hooked by Lee H. Work, Louisville, Kentucky, 2006. BILL BISHOP/IMPACT XPOZURES

Bill—Circa 1931
Second Place Readers' Choice—Adaptation
Lee H. Work

Lee Work has a favorite photograph of her husband. She fell in love with the innocent gaze of a child looking toward the future, and his blue-and-white outfit that was typical of the 1930s. She enjoys hooking fine shading and working from photographs, so it is no wonder that she chose this photograph of Bill as her subject for a rug.

Lee asked her rug hooking teacher to come up with the formula for the skin tones, and they worked together to selected a Triple Over Dye blue to white for the sailor suit. Lee chose the colors she wanted for the hair and the background. Capturing skin tones is often the biggest challenge in portraits, and this rug was no exception. The shadowing on the face gave Lee some trouble. Her rug hooking teacher had dyed an 8-value swatch for her, but Lee found that wasn't quite enough. So Lee dyed an additional five or six in-between values, which made shadowing easier.

When the rug was finished, she was pleased with how similar her rug was to that old photograph. The rug is a photograph in wool.

The Crossing, *49" x 27¹/₂", #3- and 4-cut wool on linen. Adapted from Lloyd Garrison's painting and hooked by Eloise A. Morhman, Wellington, Ohio, 2006.* BILL BISHOP/IMPACT XPOZURES

The Crossing
Third Place Readers' Choice—Adaptation
Eloise A. Mohrman

Eloise is fascinated with George Washington. When she saw the rendition of Washington's crossing the Delaware by artist Lloyd Garrison she decided to honor our country's history with a wool replica. "I am a very patriotic person," she says. "I have deep feelings for the red, white, and blue." *The Crossing*, an intricate and beautiful work of fiber art, was a project where Eloise not only used her head, but also her heart.

Eloise's wanted to capture the mood of the moment. It was icy cold in the dead of night. The ice floating in the river and winter sky in the background recall the miserable, cold winter weather endured by Washington and his troops. She used a casserole-dyed wool for the sky—she changed some of the colors from the original because she knew it would be difficult to get the same exact colors in wool. "And an artist can get finer details with his brush," she adds.

It took Eloise a year and a half to complete *The Crossing*. The artist who gave Eloise permission to use the painting called the end result "outstanding."

Celebration XVIII—2008

Emmy, *16" x 16", #3- to 6-cut wool on linen. Designed and hooked by Laura W. Pierce, Petaluma, California, 2007.* BILL BISHOP/IMPACT XPOZURES

Emmy
First Place Readers' Choice—Original Design
Laura W. Pierce

When looking for an extra special topic for a class with Michele Micarelli, Laura Pierce came across a favorite photograph. In the photo, her daughter Emma Rose was concentrating on blowing a perfect bubble. Laura knew that the challenge would be conveying the weightlessness and translucence of the bubbles.

She planned the rug's colors based on the photograph. From her previous experiences, Laura knew that she could use more colors than just skin tone for the little girl's skin. "I knew that green and purple washes are effective shadows on skin," says Laura. She manipulated the photograph using PhotoShop to decide on the colors. "My PhotoShop visual was my guide."

The biggest challenge of this project was hooking Emmy's eyes, because in the photo they are very dark. Michele helped Laura balance the light and dark in the eyes. Laura decided that she wanted the eyes to look at the bubbles. The slightly cross-eyed look is exactly the way someone would look at bubbles as they go floating away. "It moves your eye around the composition," explains Laura. "When *Emmy* was almost complete, Gertrude Callahan asked me to put one more speck of highlight in one of her eyes. Perfect!"

Laura loves the child's lips, her chubby little hands, and of course, the bubbles that catch the light. *Emmy* now blows her bubbles on a wall in Laura's family room where the portrait is a constant reminder of the innocence of childhood.

Albert Wile—Worm Digger, *28" x 31", #2- and 3-cut wool on linen. Designed and hooked by Suzanne Gunn, Centreville, Nova Scotia, Canada, 2007.*

Albert Wile—Worm Digger
Second Place Readers' Choice—Original Design
Suzanne Gunn

Suzanne Gunn keeps an eye out for interesting design ideas as she travels the Nova Scotia countryside. While on a subject-seeking foray along the Fundy Coast, Suzanne happened upon Albert Wile who was way out on the tidal flats digging for worms. With camera in hand, she hiked out to take some photos of him. But by the time she reached him, he was taking a break, sitting on his bucket, having a cigarette. "I asked if he minded if I took some photos," recalls Suzanne. "He said, 'Fine, but take them as I am.'"

Over the years, Suzanne has snapped other worm digger pictures, but the ones of Albert—even though he wasn't working at the time—turned out to be her favorites. "The photos I took of him sitting on his bucket proved to be so much more moving than the ones of him at work." The two of them chatted about his life

on the tidal flats, giving Suzanne more insight into what she wanted to convey in this rug.

Because many of her rugs are set in the same locale, Suzanne already had on hand the dyed wool she needed for the waters and beaches. Suzanne loved hooking the pants, which were covered in mud. It was a challenge to show the fabric through the mud while also showing the contours of the fabric.

Suzanne had problems figuring out the colors for the face, arms, hair, and beard. If she questioned her color choice, she ripped it out and started over, even if it was a whole week's work. In several areas, she re-hooked over and over to get the realism she wanted. The end result is an amazingly lifelike portrait in wool.

Reunion on Quince Street, *24¹/₂" x 32", #2- and 3-cut wool on linen. Designed and hooked by Lynne Fowler, Westover, Maryland, 2007.* BILL BISHOP/IMPACT XPOZURES

Reunion on Quince Street
Third Place Readers' Choice—Original Design
Lynne Fowler

Lynne Fowler's rug depicts herself and her college friends who get together every three years for a reunion, reliving old memories. Lynne takes photographs of these precious times, and this design is a compilation of several shots. Here we see three of the women walking down a ginkgo-leaf-covered street in Philadelphia. If you look very closely, you'll see Lynne peeking out from behind a tree. The autumn colors, the golden leaves, and the warm browns throughout are a wonderful snapshot of fall in Philadelphia.

Lynne planned the colors. She worked from a huge pile of golds and greens for the trees and leaves, focusing on values and small shapes, trying to make the natural elements of the rug appear impressionistic and warm. The dark building to the right of the figures was a challenge. Lynne discovered it was difficult to imply structure. Rather than considering it as one object, she broke it down into small sections and hooked each section one value at a time.

She loves the intimacy of these good friends who shared a wonderful time in life together, and she loves the implied motion in the rug as the women stroll down the street during their reunion. The rug now hangs in the entry hall of Lynne's new studio space, beckoning people to come in and share their own memories.

Leopard, *21" x 21", #3- and 4-cut wool on rug warp. Designed by Jon Ciemiewicz; hooked by Judy A. Carter, Willow Street, Pennsylvania, 2007.* BILL BISHOP/IMPACT XPOZURES

Leopard
First Place Readers' Choice—Commercial Design
Judy A. Carter

Judy Carter is a long-time rug hooker with more than 80 completed projects to her credit. She designs her own patterns and tackles commercial projects as well. This rug was a natural choice for Judy: she already hooked close-up rugs of a lion and tiger—projects she found dramatic and fun. *Leopard* fit into the series, and she liked that the design incorporated more of the body of the animal.

Judy prefers using textures and fine cuts of wool to capture the realistic look of animals. This rug was no exception. The most

challenging part of this rug was the big cat's paw. "There isn't much contrast in the paw, so it's hard to make it look realistic," says Judy. Judy discovered that concentrating on the dark spots for contrast made it much easier to capture the realism.

Judy finished the rug with cording, whipped with Persian wool yarn. She attached one side of the rug tape while she whipstitched it so she only had to hand sew one side of tape. "This gives a smoother finish," she says.

Poppy Seed, *28" x 43", #3-cut wool on linen. Designed by Heirloom Rugs; hooked by Peggy Hannum, Lancaster, Pennsylvania, 2006.*
BILL BISHOP/IMPACT XPOZURES

Poppy Seed
Second Place Readers' Choice—Commercial Design
Peggy Hannum

Peggy Hannum has been creating rug art for more than 30 years. During that time she has completed many rugs, using many different styles and various cuts of wool. This rug, *Poppy Seed*, appealed to her because of the fine tapestry hooking and the colorful and vivacious flower motifs. Peggy is an avid gardener and liked how the spring flowers "pop out" from the leaves in an array of vivid colors, from white to red.

This pattern from Heirloom Rugs was a perfect fit for Peggy. She sent Nancy Blood pictures of her poppies, and Nancy returned color formulas to match what she saw in the pictures. Nancy color planned the rug, and instructed Peggy in pleating and ruffling the petals, which was a technique that Peggy had never tried before.

The sprigs of wheat were the most challenging aspects of the design. Peggy hooked them with a #2-cut wool to capture the feathery look. She outlined each of the grains with one thread of wool so that they did not all become one indistinguishable mass.

While the full-bloom flowers in *Poppy Seed* catch the viewer's eye, the rug shows poppies in various stages of growth. "I had

almost finished the rug when a friend asked, 'Where are the seeds?'" recalls Peggy. "I had interpreted several indistinguishable blobs as buds, so I regrouped and made them seeds, which is no doubt what they were supposed to be." She learned an important lesson: to pay attention to the name of a rug.

Big Blue at Sunset, *36" x 36", #4-cut hand-dyed wool on monk's cloth. Designed by Pam Chase; hooked by Millie Parks, Dover, New Hampshire, 2006.* BILL BISHOP/IMPACT XPOZURES

Big Blue at Sunset
Third Place Readers' Choice—Commercial Design
Millie Parks

Millie Parks of Dover, New Hampshire, loves to watch great blue herons along the Bellamy River where she lives. "This is a tidal river and blue herons are frequent visitors," she explains. "I love to watch these majestic birds. And our house faces west, so we enjoy many fabulous sunsets. I wanted a rug with one large bird and some of the details of our backyard on the water." *Big Blue at Sunset* combines both of these, with a majestic sunset thrown in.

It was a challenge to capture the light reflecting off the water and the bird. She particularly liked working on the head of the bird surrounded by the colors of the sunset. The play of light within the rug made her aware of the importance of how light

hits objects. "I'm ready to take on another challenge, perhaps another bird-type original rug," Millie says. Millie enjoyed working with the reflections, the sky, and the bird itself.

Hooking this rug pushed Millie beyond the beginner level and opened her eyes to the possibilities of using wool to create art. She thanks rug hooking for bringing her into a whole new world of design and color. Even though she's never taken any formal art classes, Millie is much more aware of color combinations. Through her teacher, Angela Foote, Millie learned about balance and learned to be a little more daring in her color creations.

Roche Harbor Tulips in Wool, *23^1/$_2$″ x 31^1/$_2$″, #6-cut wool on linen. Adapted from Kristy Gjesme's watercolor painting and hooked by Arleen Mauger, Lancaster, Pennsylvania, 2007.*
BILL BISHOP/IMPACT XPOZURES

Roche Harbor Tulips in Wool
Third Place Readers' Choice—Adaptation
Arleen Mauger

The idea for this rug came about while Arleen and her husband were sailing the San Juan Islands of Washington State and came into a town called Roche Harbor. Craftsmen and artists were selling their creative work, and Arleen noticed a watercolor painting by Kristy Gjesme entitled *Roche Harbor Tulips.* "It was the blend of colors that attracted me to this design, as well as the memories of that sailing trip," Arleen recalls. "We could see so many flowers from our boat slip in Roche Harbor."

Arleen purchased the print and asked Kristy, the artist, if she could make it into a rug, a question that was met with an immediate yes. Arleen stayed true to Kristy's art in the colors she used for the rug. She wanted to duplicate the wool shades from the watercolor painting, which turned out to be Arleen's biggest challenge. She really wanted the rug to have that watercolor look, and finding wools to match the original print colors was difficult. Through her experimenting, Arleen learned new ways to dye wool. "Dyeing fascinates me and I enjoy learning new techniques. I hope to find more time to experiment with dyeing in the future." And deciding what direction to hook for various parts of the design was a challenge because she wanted the design to have depth and dimension. She learned that the direction in which she hooked determined if a section stood out or blended in.

Gently Down the Stream, *22" x 34", #3- and 6-cut wool on monk's cloth. Adapted from a Pine Island Primitives' commercial pattern and hooked by Juanita Darnold, Hot Springs Village, Arkansas, 2007.* BILL BISHOP/IMPACT XPOZURES

Gently Down the Stream
Second Place Readers' Choice—Adaptation
Juanita Darnold

Juanita Darnold was captivated by this colorful and whimsical image the minute a friend purchased it as a pattern. Her friend asked Juanita if she was interested in the challenge of hooking the design. Since Juanita didn't have any other projects going on at the time, she decided to give *Gently Down the Stream* a try.

Juanita used a copy of the original antique postcard that came with the pattern for color planning. By pure coincidence, she received a huge box of wool with many cut swatches and colors. She used one of the swatches for the boat, starting at both ends and working toward the middle so she could get the green she wanted on the front end. She spot dyed some Cushing blue for the sky, and aqua over various whites for the water.

The rabbit required shading, fingering, and reverse hooking in order to get it right, but the most challenging aspect of the design was the boat and the dark chick. As Juanita hooked, she learned a lot about animal fur and feather shading and the methods used to make it appear as realistic as possible. But most of all, she learned that she really loved hooking animals and fine cut detail work.

The rug is displayed on a wall in Juanita's bedroom. She used

sewing needles to hang it so she can easily put it up or take it down as needed. Eventually, it will be on its way to Texas for a new grandson.

For They Love Their Children Too, *24³/4" x 29¹/4", recycled and re-dyed nylons on rug warp. Adapted from Michael Neugebauer's photo (with permission) and hooked by Patti Armstrong, Zurich, Ontario, Canada, 2007.* BILL BISHOP/IMPACT XPOZURES

For They Love Their Children Too
Third Place Readers' Choice—Adaptation

Patti Armstrong

Rug hooker Patti Armstrong was working on a series of 24 rugs about mothers and daughters when she decided to show not only human mothers and daughters, but animal moms and kids as well. Patti admired the work of animal advocate Jane Goodall and knew she had found her subject when she came across a photograph of a mother and her baby in Goodall's book *Chimpanzees That I Love.* "When I saw it, I had to use it," recalls Patti, "because it shows this animal affectionately cradling her baby, lovingly looking down at it. *For They Love Their Children Too* was the perfect addition to her series.

Patti hooked the entire rug using recycled and new factory-seconds nylon stockings that she dyed herself. Her favorite part of the

rug is the expressions on the chimps' faces—they show how much the mother genuinely loves her baby. "You can see it, feel it," Patti says. "The baby looks directly at the observer; her eyes are inquisitive, expressive." The most challenging section was the mother's hand. Patti had to make the fingers look leathery, like skin, while making the back of her hand look furry. She used the direction of the hooking to accomplish this daunting task.

Patti plans on eventually photographing and publishing in book form all the rugs she has created in her mothers and daughters series. "It's been an emotional, exciting journey so far," she says. "I am thrilled to be able to honor and celebrate these mothers."

R·U·G HOOKING
MARKETPLACE

Hooked Rug Landscapes

Whether you enjoy hooking realistic or impressionistic landscapes, you'll be sure to find this new book from *Rug Hooking* magazine invaluable. Throughout *Hooked Rug Landscapes,* author Anne-Marie Littenberg, will guide you step-by-step through the process of designing and hooking a landscape. She combines the craft of rug hooking with basic art skills used for centuries. This beautiful book will guide you through the inspiration, design, and planning stages of your rug. Includes chapters on perspective, contrast, and color. **Price: $24.95*** **(Shipping & Handling is $4.95 U.S. & $6.95 Canadian)**

Creating an Antique Look in Hand-Hooked Rugs

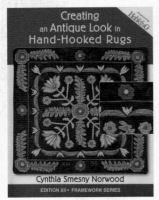

One of the most popular requests of rug hookers today is how to achieve the antique look in hand-hooked rugs. In response to that, *Rug Hooking* magazine is pleased to bring you, *Creating an Antique Look in Hand-Hooked Rugs* written by Cynthia Norwood, a frequent contributor to the magazine. From start to finish, the book will guide you through the details of basic design elements for creating an antique look. This book also includes a FREE full-size pull-out primitive rug pattern. **Price: $19.95*** **(Shipping & Handling is $4.95 U.S. & $6.95 Canadian)**

The Rug Hooker's Bible

For over 30 years, Jane Olson has taught rug-hooking to rug hookers of all levels—beginners to advanced. Now in this collaborative effort with Gene Shepherd, comes a clear, concise "Bible" for the novice as well as the seasoned hooker. This beautifully illustrated book, written in an easy-to-read format, will open the door to the art of rug hooking. You won't want to be without it! **Price: $29.95*** **(Shipping & Handling is $4.95 U.S. & $6.95 Canadian)**

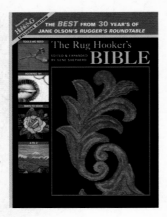

Learn At Home DVD Series

For even more help and guidance with rug hooking, we invite you to purchase the *"Learn at Home DVD Series"* with your teacher Gene Shepherd. See different methods in intricate detail, repeat sections at the push of a button (as often as you wish), or freeze-frame any section for your intimate review. These DVDs are designed to serve as an instructional DVD for Chapters 2 and 3 of *The Rug Hooker's Bible.* Bring hooking lessons to the comfort of your home! DVD Vol. 1 (Hooking 101) and DVD Vol. 2 (Multiple Ways to Hook) **Price: $17.95 per DVD or $35.90 for both*** **(Shipping & Handling is $4.95 U.S. & $6.95 Canadian)**

Pictorial Hooked Rugs

One of the most challenging of all rug styles is the pictorial rug or wall hanging. In *Rug Hooking*'s newest book, *Pictorial Hooked Rugs,* well-known rug hooker and author, Jane Halliwell Green guides the reader through the process of how to create pictorial rugs from start to finish. The full-color book is the definitive instructional manual on how to create the elements of a pictorial rug. *Pictorial Hooked Rugs* contains tips and tricks to take the guesswork out of planning a personalized rug, along with a FREE full-size pattern project. This book is an essential tool for those who wish to hook pictorial designs. **Price: $24.95*** **(Shipping & Handling is $4.95 U.S. & $6.95 Canadian)**

Pattern Designs for Rug Hookers

Pattern Designs for Rug Hookers features 15 projects designed by well-known rug hooking artisans. Each project includes designers' tips for creating a wide-cut primitive look, along with detailed step-by-step directions and easy-to-follow text. You'll also receive free pattern line drawings with material lists for each project. *Pattern Designs for Rug Hookers* is filled with all types of projects, from rugs and pillows to wall hangings, table runners, and more. **Price: $19.95*** (Shipping & Handling is $4.95 U.S. & $6.95 Canadian)

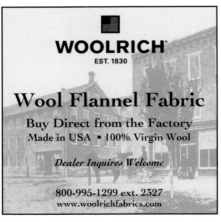